THE BEGINNERS' GUIDE TO
TRACING YOUR ROOTS

"A fascinating and informative book. Diane Marelli vividly describes her search through previous generations. Despite the general supposition that 'one's own family is of scant [interest]', her painstaking attention to detail [regarding] the Census is utterly absorbing. [The] photographs become alive as she [describes the] discovery of the certificates, [particularly] those in the ever crowded marriage [I would] recommend Mrs Marelli's book [as reading] to anyone wishing to trace [their antecedents." **Lady Cleaver**

"I found researching my own family history fascinating. I recommend you read Diane's book so that you too can find out about your ancestors." **Rufus Sewell**

"This book is written in a refreshing style not often found in family history books. It reveals the enthusiasm and passion that someone can acquire from family history research. Diane Marelli's book cannot fail to instil in anyone the interest to pursue their family history. Hopefully her readers will produce their family histories in an equally interesting and enthusiastic manner." **Robert Blatchford**, Editor of *The Family and Local History Handbook*, 8th edition. www.genealogical.co.uk

In memory of

Albert William Marelli
(1915 – 1998)
&
Charles Moloney
(1888 – 1976)
&
Harry William Reynolds
(1940 – 2001)

Dedicated to my mother

Lilian Margaret Hughes, previously Moloney, née Reynolds

howto**books**

Please send for a free copy of the latest catalogue to:
How To Books, Springhill House, Springhill Road, Begbroke, Oxford OX5 1RX
email: info@howtobooks.co.uk
http://www.howtobooks.co.uk

REVISED AND UPDATED
SECOND EDITION

THE BEGINNERS' GUIDE TO
TRACING YOUR ROOTS

AN INSPIRATIONAL
AND ENCOURAGING
INTRODUCTION TO
DISCOVERING YOUR
FAMILY'S PAST...

DIANE MARELLI

howtobooks

Published by How To Books Ltd,
Springhill House, Springhill Road, Begbroke
Oxford OX5 1RX. United Kingdom.
Tel: (01865) 375794. Fax: (01865) 379162
info@howtobooks.co.uk
www.howtobooks.co.uk

First edition published 2003
Reprinted 2004
Reprinted 2006
Second edition 2007

British Library Cataloguing in Publication Data.
A catalogue record for this book is available from the British Library.

Cover design by Baseline Arts Ltd, Oxford
Produced for How To Books by Deer Park Productions, Tavistock
Typeset and design by Baseline Arts Ltd, Oxford
Printed and bound in Great Britain, by Cromwell Press Ltd, Trowbridge, Wiltshire

NOTE: The material contained in this book is set out in good faith for general
guidance and no liability can be accepted for loss or expense incurred as a result
of relying in particular circumstances on statements made in this book. Laws and
regulations are complex and liable to change, and readers should check the current
position with the relevant authorities before making personal arrangements.

Contents

Acknowledgements

Some material in this publication is reprinted by permission of the Church of Jesus Christ of Latter-Day Saints. In granting permission for this use of copyrighted material, the Church does not imply endorsement or authorisation of this publication.

Birth, marriage and death certificates from the Office of National Statistics are © Crown copyright and reproduced with the permission of the Controller of HMSO and the Queen's Printer for Scotland.

Special thanks must go to Wendy Bevan, my employer but also my friend, for her all her support. And a great big thank you to all my friends and family, especially my husband Brian for putting up with me during my genealogical journey.

On Tuesday, 27 May 2003, we received the sad news that the lovely Ann Gosling had passed away unexpectedly. Her husband Ron had died in 2001. We remain in contact with their two children Keith and Jane. (See Chapter 5, March 2001.)

Introduction

My eyes open to a swath of light blazing across the darkness of my bedroom as the sound of a car roars off into the night, and my heart thuds cruelly; it is not William. Why is he ignoring me? I cannot go on alone, I need his help, yet he refuses again and again to listen. I cannot believe he would do this especially after all I have done for him, introducing him into the family, making him part of our lives. Yet this is how he repays me by ignoring me. Well I hope he is pleased with himself. Sleepless nights, headaches and tears are what I am reduced to and why? Because William Podevin born circa 1800 refuses to step out of his spirit world into mine and tell me **'Where the hell he was born!'**

If only it were that simple...

When I look back over my four, very basic, years of tracing both mine and my husband's family history, I cannot express the frustrations experienced in attempting to track down that elusive ancestor nor the joy felt discovering an ancestor that was long forgotten, or never known about. Never could I have imagined the seesaw of emotion I would undergo finding the birth of an ancestor one week to discover the next that he or she had died tragically young, or revealing surprising second marriages or marriages that never happened, or uncovering French connections that were always thought of as fantasy. And I will always remember the uncanny sensation of finding out that when I moved from one end of the country to the other I had unknowingly been walking in the footsteps of my ancestors for years.

Family research is exhilarating, especially when a puzzle comes together. It is like being a detective but without the help of witnesses. There are still many family skeletons and intrigues that drive me mad and that may never be resolved but I cannot give up trying. I am hooked and yet I have only just begun.

As a complete beginner – and in the world of family history I still am – I searched for a book to help *me* with my research, a book that I could relate to on a basic level, but they all seemed so advanced with so much information that I could not take it all in, although I now admit I find them invaluable. I was a lonely researcher and needed a friend to consult with, someone who was sharing the same experiences and aggravations that I was.

All of a sudden other potential family historians, in the same dilemma that I was in four years ago, started asking me questions. How did I start? Where did I find all my information? How did I find the time to carry out all the research? What did I do when I got 'genealogist's block'? How did I store everything? Did I want to give up at times? What mistakes did I make?

Now, when I hear 'there is no point researching my family, they are so boring,' I am horrified. How do they know? I was guilty of the same misconception about my own family initially; how wrong I was. That is when I decided to write about my experiences and findings, as basic as they are, because I owe it to my ancestors. They struggled through difficult times to survive and if they had not would I be here to write about it today?

I suppose, if I was honest, I would class myself as a naturally impatient individual that attacks projects with lots of energy and tenacity but with very little thought. If there is any truth in the saying 'we learn by our mistakes' then you might be forgiven for thinking that I have learned a lot after four years of research. To some extent I have, but do I continue to make the same mistakes? Yes, infuriatingly. Why? Because there is so much to think about and so little time when making that special day trip to the 'Family Manic Centre' in London, more commonly known as the 'Family Record Centre', or similar organisations.

Although I carried out the majority of my physical research alone I have needed help on certain issues and found there are people out there willing to assist – all you have to do is ask. I have been and still am continually grateful for the kindness of strangers via forums on the Internet or from institutions, history centres and people just wanting to help.

As with many family historians my search began with the death of a close relative, my father-in-law Albert William Marelli in 1998, so that is where I will start.

Diane Marelli

The Beginning
(June to July 1998)

ALBERT WILLIAM MARELLI, KNOWN TO MOST AS BERT, is of Italian extraction, a fact that I found very interesting and romantic so you would assume, naturally, that I delved into Bert's life story and those of his ancestors often. Wrong! Now Bert has gone taking with him a million unanswered questions and to add to my frustration, my husband, Brian, is just as guilty of the same negligence towards his family history as I am. Bert did not talk very much about his past, except for the story about his grandfather Martino who walked from Italy and started his life in England selling ice off the back of wagons. Why did Bert talk so little about his background I now ask myself? Was it because he was reluctant to divulge very much information or because we failed to listen or show deeper interest by asking questions? Whatever Bert's reasons I was horrified that Brian knew so little, while I could be forgiven as I was only the daughter-in-law. *I now admit, somewhat reluctantly, that it took me another two years to realise I knew even less about my own family history than Brian knew about his.*

June 1998 – Bert's papers

Brian inherited lots of paperwork and family photographs from Bert and among the piles were some very interesting documents:

1. An extract from the Marriage Register for Martino Marelli (Bert's grandfather) to Amy Plummer. Witnesses present were William and Susan Plummer. It also told us that Martino lived in Lower Marsh, Lambeth at this time and is the son of Angelino Marelli and that Amy Plummer is from Tooting and the daughter of William Plummer. They were married on Christmas Day, 1891. *So we not only had*

EXTRACT TRANSLATED FROM THE MARRIAGE REGISTER KEPT AT

ST. GEORGE'S CATHEDRAL, SOUTHWARK, LONDON.

In the year 18 *91* on the *Twenty fifth* day of *December* *David Maloney* *Martino Marelli* living at *Lower Marsh Lambeth* Son of *Angelino Marell*

AND

my Plummer living at *Tooting Surrey* Daughter of *William Plumm*

Witnesses Present | *William Plummer* *Susan Plummer*

I Certify that the above is a correct Translation from the Latin Original.

Given at St. George's, this *29* — day of *June* 18 *97* —by me, *Thomas B* Sacristan.

1.1 Extract of marriage for Martino and Amy

Martino's marriage certificate but the name of his father, Amy's maiden name, the name of her father, William Plummer, and presumably the name of Amy's mother, Susan Plummer, who is a witness at the wedding. Also the marriage extract is dated 29 June 1897, six years after the marriage took place so they must have ordered this extra copy for a reason.

2. The death certificate dated 13 February 1940 for Martino Marelli, aged 88. He was living at Battersea, and present at his death was his daughter M. Davies of Battersea. The cause of death is given as heart failure, gastric haemorrhage (*sic*) and cancer of the colon. *This gave us the married surname of one of Martino's daughters, Davies.*

3. The birth certificate for Lilian Lucretia Chappell, Bert's mother, dated 10 April 1892, living in Lyme Regis, Dorset. Her parents were listed as Frederick Stone Chappell and Susan Chappell formerly Lugg. The occupation of Lilian's father is given as a painter (journeyman). *We now had two sets of great grandparents.*

4. The birth certificate for Albert Marelli, son of Martino and Amy (father to Bert and grandfather to Brian), who was born exactly one year to the day that his parents married, Christmas Day, 1892. This certificate told me that Martino and Amy were living at Martino's address as Lower Marsh. The certificate also gave us an occupation for Martino of master fishmonger. *We had heard stories of Martino owning fish and chip shops.* On the back of this copy of the birth certificate is National Insurance information dated 20 May 1912, after the Act had come into being in 1911. *So this copy of the birth certificate was also ordered for a reason.*

5. The marriage certificate for Albert Marelli dated 25 July 1912, aged 19 of Battersea, occupation motor mechanic, and Lilian Lucretia Chappell, aged 20 of the same address, no occupation. It also states that Martino is Albert's father together with his occupation, fishmonger, and also that Frederick Stone Chappell is Lilian's father with his occupation, carpenter. Witnesses were R. G. Spiller and Rosa Spiller. They were married in Wandsworth Register Office. *Perhaps this forthcoming marriage was the reason Albert ordered a copy of his birth certificate.*

6. The death certificate for Albert Marelli, dated 13 July 1974, aged 81. This gave his occupation as carpenter (retired) and his home address at Chertsey. Present at his death were Albert William Marelli – Bert, of East Molesey. The cause of death was given as left ventricular failure, myocardia infarct (*sic*).

7. Incredibly there is a document dated October 1906 from the Diocese of Milan, signed by Rev. Giovanni Villa, Reverend of Milan Foundlings Home (see figure 1.2). The document states that Martino Antonio Merelli (*sic*), parents unknown, was born on 20 January 1852 and baptised the same day. *So in 1906 someone else in the family had tried to locate Martino's birth details.*

8. Of most interest is a Certificate of Naturalisation dated 17 May 1897 relating to Martino, who was then aged 44 years, married and still living in Lower Marsh but at a different

1.2 Letter from the Diocese of Milan

address (see figure 1.3). The naturalisation certificate also listed his children: Helen aged 20, Martin aged 17, Ada aged 15, Matilda aged 12, Albert aged 3 and Amelia aged 1. *Although naturalisation took place in May 1897 the marriage extract for Martino and Amy was ordered in June of the same year. Perhaps the original copy was mislaid during the application for British citizenship. I wonder if the M. Davies who was present at Martino's death is Matilda?*

1.3 Naturalisation certificate for Martino Marelli

We were completely fascinated by the above but also puzzled because four of the children listed on the naturalisation certificate were born prior to Martino's marriage to Amy Plummer. There had never been any discussion within the family of Martino having been married twice. *Surely someone would have known this?* For a few days we assumed that either Amy had been married before and that her children took the name Marelli when she married Martino or that maybe Amy and Martino had lived together before marriage for some reason. We even discussed these possibilities with Brian's only aunt and uncle (Vic and Bet) but they could not help. As far as the family was concerned Martino only married once and they had heard nothing to the contrary. We came to the conclusion that we had to investigate this further and decided to find a birth certificate for the oldest named child of Martino called Helen, as named on the naturalisation certificate, in the hope that this certificate would furnish us with a clue.

With all of the above we noted that Martino, Albert and Bert, three generations of Marelli men, lived into their 80s and we could now go back four generations on a couple of branches of Brian's family tree (see figure 1.4).

1.4 Brian's Ancestors

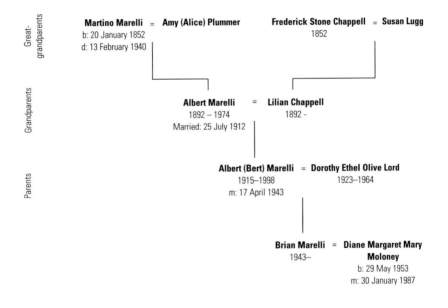

Brian's Ancestors – July 1998

The first important piece of information we found out is that Somerset House no longer held births, marriages and deaths! *When did this happen?* We discovered the existence of the Family Record Centre (FRC), London and set out to find Helen, one of the mysterious older children of Martino Marelli, Brian's great grandfather, prior to his marriage to Amy Plummer in 1891. We made the decision to unravel this mystery in memory of Bert, because at that time we had no real interest in family history ourselves. To be honest we did not have a clue about family history or how to go about it but felt it would be interesting to solve this riddle.

We did not arrive at the FRC until about 11.30 a.m. on a Saturday morning mainly because we had to catch a train into London and two tubes followed by a 20-minute walk. We had our bags searched by security and were directed downstairs where there are facilities, lockers, snack machines, phones and a large seating area. Back upstairs through reception on the right we found the area housing all the registers of Births, Marriages and Deaths, plus an enquiry desk. Within this area are masses of shelves housing the large index volumes all stacked in rows with large sloping desks placed between the rows to rest the books on while researching. The place was heaving with people that day and everyone seemed to know what they were doing except for us, but the atmosphere was exhilarating. After queuing at the information desk we were directed to Births and looked at the years surrounding 1876 to 1878 when Helen, if the age is correct on the naturalisation certificate, is supposed to have been born. We found nothing registered under the name Helen Marelli. To our dismay we also discovered our first mistake, we had only looked at one volume for each year instead of four. What we failed to take in at this point is that there are four books for every year split into quarters.

Convinced we would now find Helen we started again but failed to find her although we did find a birth for a Rosa Marelli, born in 1877 in Islington, and Martin Marelli born in 1878 in Lambeth, a thrilling experience. We went for a coffee and thought about things. Is Helen the illegitimate daughter of Amy? Is she adopted? Is she perhaps Martino's daughter from a previous relationship? Confusion fogged our minds so we decided to look for some of the other children. Sadly in our eagerness to get to the FRC we had not taken with us one vital piece of information, the naturalisation document listing the names and ages of Martino's children, but then we only ever intended to look for Helen!

Completely unequipped we searched through births again from 1876 and located two more in the London area and one in Manchester. *Perhaps the birth in Manchester is a relative of Martino's?* The children we found were Ada in 1880 and Matilda in 1882, both from Lambeth. The Macclesfield birth was for a John Fred. We had no idea if any of these finds were related to Martino but suddenly we had to find out. It occurred to us that even though we could not find Helen Marelli we had found other children so this meant that Martino had been in a relationship previously!

Energised we rushed back to customer services with our precious discoveries to ask how we order the certificates only to be told we had not taken down enough information and needed to take a pink form and fill in all the details from the registers.

Eventually, after revisiting the same volumes for the third time, we collected all the necessary information, queued and ordered all four certificates.

Our next visit was to the Marriage indexes. *Well we couldn't leave now, not without looking for Martino's first wife, could we, if indeed he had married before his marriage to Amy?* As his eldest child, Helen, was 20 in 1897 we began our search four years prior to her probable birth date from the year 1873 with every intention to continue until 1897, the extra years were to allow room for error.

With a scrap of paper and pencil ready to note each year and quarter methodically we grabbed a volume each, fighting for a space in this very popular area for family historians. I wanted everyone to disappear and leave us alone to carry out our most important research; no one else could be doing anything as vital as we were! So I was pleased that although I am reasonably petite I am quite strong and able to squeeze into little gaps, duck under arms and swing heavy index volumes onto desks with agility. I was getting quite hot and bothered thinking it was going to get rough but managed to keep my irritation in check when Brian grabbed me by the shoulder and turned me round to face him. Wordlessly he pointed to the name of his great grandfather Martino Marelli in the first quarter of 1875 and for one rare moment I too was speechless. It was staggering, our eyes filled with tears; it was as if we had just stepped back in time and said, 'Hello, Martino'. What would Martino have made of us doing this 123 years after his marriage and 48 years after his death, we wondered in amazement? We ordered this certificate but as we were mentally drained, hungry and emotional we decided to head home and digest what we had found along with some sandwiches.

Where to begin

My friend Lisa Castle, née Garbett, asked me a question recently. She said: 'If I went to the place where all the records of Births are kept where would I start and what would I look for?'

I thought about it for a moment, assuming she would have information about her grandparents, and said, 'Your great grandparents probably.'

And she replied, 'But I don't even have any information about my grandparents who are both dead. So where do I start looking and how would I know if I had found the right ancestor? How can anyone be sure they have found the right ancestors?'

This is how I explained it to her.

A birth certificate of a grandparent will give you the names of your great grandparents on one branch of your family tree. So as she did not have her grandfather's birth certificate I asked her if she knew the year her grandfather died and his age at the time of death. He died in 1964, she believed, aged about 58 years in Southampton but she did not know his actual birth date.

I suggested she first search for his death certificate. This should give her his age at death or date of birth enabling her to look for his birth details. As she only had an approximate age and year she would need to search the years surrounding 1964 for the district of Southampton. I then suggested she could try and source his marriage certificate but she had no information about when he was married or her grandmother's maiden name or the place they were married. This would mean searching records over many years but the thought of this was too daunting for her at this stage. However, as we could find an approximate year of birth we decided this would be her next step.

Assuming she had acquired the death certificate that only gave his age as 58 years this would give us an approximate birth year of 1906. I say approximate because he could have been nearly 59 years old at the time of his death, so he could have been born in 1905, or if born in the December of 1906 he may not have been registered until 1907. To be safe she would need to search the three years 1905, 1906 and 1907. If she does not find him in those three years then she needs to widen her search each side and look in 1904 and 1908 and so on. (It is possible her grandfather could be mistaken about his age or the person registering the death could have given incorrect information, both very common problems in family research.)

I then asked whether she knew where her grandfather lived as a child. She told me that her parents used to talk about Pontypool in Wales.

If we assume this information is correct we now have Pontypool as the district he was born and the approximate year of birth, 1905–1907.

Her grandfather's name was Edgar Garbett. This is a good name as it is not as common as, say, Walker, but to be on the safe side I asked if he had any other names. She did not think so but rumour had it he was a twin and she thought the twin's name was Ivor but was not entirely sure. The twin element in her search would be a main clue if faced with a choice of Edgar Garbetts born in Pontypool in the years she is searching. I also explained that if she could not find Edgar in the three search years or surrounding years then he might have been christened with a different Christian name and Edgar could be his second name. So she would also need to look under all the Garbetts with second names of Edgar or with a second initial of E as sometimes people chose to use their middle names through life. Also he could have another middle name and be listed as George Edgar F. Garbett or something similar in the registers at the FRC. But her main clue would be to find two Garbetts with the same registration information if Edgar was in fact a twin.

So by asking a few questions we found the following:

Approximate year of birth:	1905–1907
Place of birth/district:	Pontypool, Wales
Name:	Edgar Garbett
	Edgar ? Garbett
or...	? Edgar Garbett
or...	? Edgar F. Garbett or similar
Main clue:	A possible twin called Ivor

If she did not find the birth certificate of her grandfather in the years above we will have to assume that he was younger or older and widen the search or consider other districts near to Pontypool. If faced with more than one possibility for Edgar Garbett and no twin, then without further clues she may well have to order several certificates starting with the most likely one until she finds her grandfather, or try locating a marriage certificate. If she finds what she believes to be her grandfather's birth certificate, that will name his father and occupation and also his mother, including her maiden name. She can then search for her great grandparents. Or if she did not find what she believed to be the correct birth certificate then the marriage certificate for her grandfather would still be the next step. The marriage certificate will name his father and in turn confirm she has the correct birth certificate. Before embarking on this search she needs to question family members and try to ascertain where her grandfather was living at the time of his marriage, his wife's maiden name and the age of their children if possible. She would then choose a date to start her search prior to the age of their oldest child or from an age when her grandfather could have married.

It is always advisable to begin your search for an ancestor's particular birth, marriage or death certificate or for the certificate for which you have the most clues.

This may not seem much information to the novice researcher but I can promise you there will be times during your research that you will be grateful for a third of the above information to go on!

So remember if any of your relatives have birth, marriage or death certificates of family members ask if you can take copies now. It will not only speed up your research but will save you time and expense when you are ready to start your own research. Also ask questions about grandparents, aunts and uncles: their ages, place of birth, middle names, maiden names and childhood memories. And write it all down because one day something in your notes could solve one of many problems you are guaranteed to encounter in this frustrating business.

When hoping to find certificates for your ancestors it is important to note that Civil Registration began in England and Wales in 1837 so you will not be able to find certificates prior to this date. When searching through Birth, Marriage and Death registers remember that each year is split into four quarters and all details are listed alphabetically so there could be several volumes for each quarter depending on the number of births, deaths or marriages at that time. January, February and March are listed under March. April, May and June are under June. July, August and September are under September. October, November and December are under December.

At the FRC the registers for Births, Marriages and Deaths are colour coded. The indexes of Births are housed in red books. The indexes of Marriages are housed in green books and the indexes of Deaths are housed in black books. You cannot view the actual certificate at the FRC – you can only view the indexes here but can order a certificate once you have the correct index information. At other establishments the indexes will be housed on microfiche. When ordering certificates at the FRC you will be required to fill in a corresponding colour-coded form: pink for ordering Birth certificates, green for ordering Marriage certificates, and mauve for ordering Death certificates. Certificates usually take about a week, sometimes a little longer by post, but you can arrange to collect your certificate in person within four days. There is also a facility to arrange collection of a certificate within 24 hours but the cost is about £22.50.

The forms are very easy to use and each certificate costs £7.00, but it is important to ensure you record the correct information from the registers. The minimum information you will require from the register to order a birth certificate for instance is the **surname at birth, forenames, date or year of birth.** The **quarter** and the **district** the birth is registered under, and the **Volume**, i.e. 2a, and the **page number** that follows the volume number in the register.

For example:

Name	DOB	Quarter	District	Vol.	Page
John Albert Williams	1906	September	Kingston	2a	391

You can order certificates while at the FRC, or at a later date by phone from the General Register Office (GRO) in Southport. The cost varies if ordering by phone via the GRO depending on whether you have the register information as above, or just a name and a date. If you are unsure of the date you can request a five-year search for an individual. For further information about services provided by the GRO telephone: 0870 2437788.

The Family Records Centre is located at 1 Myddelton Street, Islington, London, EC1R 1UW, tel: 0208 392 5300. Their website is www.familyrecords.gov.uk. The FRC holds information for **England** and **Wales** including Birth, Marriage and Death registers and Census Returns for 1841, 1851, 1861, 1871, 1881, 1891 and 1901 (more about the Census returns later). There are other places you can view microfiche registers of Births, Marriages and Deaths for England and Wales such as the Central Library in Liverpool. Your local history centre may also hold records for your area or you can order a search and certificate, if you have the relevant information, via your local Registrar Office or via other Registrar Offices countrywide.

Please note that changes have been made to the Indexes: Births from September 1911 now show the maiden name of the mother. Marriages from March 1912 show the surname of the spouse. Deaths from March 1866 to March 1969 the age at death is shown and from June 1969 the date of birth is shown. Census records can be viewed by a payable resource online via Ancestry.com and findmypast.com. If you are visiting the FRC you can gain free access online to Ancestry.com records. You can also gain full access to BMDs via subscription with: www.findmypast.com and www.ancestry.co.uk, or free with www.freebmd.org.uk – a great resource, although incomplete at this date in time, records are added almost daily; a great resource if looking for ancestors from 1837 to about 1910.

Scotland Civil registration was introduced in 1855 and all birth, marriage and death certificates are held by the General Register Office for Scotland. For births, marriages and deaths that took place more than 100 years ago you can view indexes on the Internet via www.scotlandspeople.gov.uk. You will be charged for viewing these indexes. There is also Census information and Old Parish Registers of baptisms and marriages.

Ireland Births and deaths are held from 1864 and marriages from 1845 at the General Register Office of Northern Ireland. Full details are on their website www.groni.gov.uk.

The first certificates arrived

The first batch of certificates arrived on the following Friday morning. *I was to learn that certificates could take longer depending on demand.* I held the unopened envelope in my hand marvelling at what secrets of the past it would reveal, relishing the moment, then sat on the floor and ripped it open.

The first birth was for Rosa, dated 27 August 1877, daughter of Martino Marelli, a carman and Ellen Marelli formerly McDonald, living in Islington (see figure 1.5). *It is true, Martino had been married before and at that moment I was the only living Marelli that knew this amazing piece of information. I felt so proud of Brian and myself; we had done this amazing thing. Wow!*

1.5 Rosa Marelli – birth certificate

1.6 Martin Marelli – birth certificate

The second birth was for Martin, dated 29 August 1878, giving an address in Lambeth, the father Martino, occupation carman and mother Ellen Marelli, formerly Mackdonald (*sic*) (see figure 1.6).

The third birth was for Ada, dated 23 June 1880, giving an address of Waterloo, occupation of father, ice merchant, mother Ellen Marelli formerly Mackdonald.

The fourth birth was for Matilda, dated 10 October 1882 and giving yet another address in Lambeth, occupation of father, carman again, mother Ellen Marelli, formerly Mackdonald.

The fifth birth was for a John Fred from Macclesfield, whose father was George Joseph, occupation railway clerk, and mother Mary, formerly Worthington. *This appeared to be from a different family. We would have to investigate further.*

Last but by far the most exciting certificate was the marriage certificate for Martino. Dated 1 February 1875 it gave Martino's age as 23 years, occupation carman, living in Holborn. It stated his father's name as Martino and his occupation as carman (see figure 1.7). *(How strange – on the extract of his marriage to Amy it gives the father's name as Angelino.)* Martino's first wife was Ellen McDonald, aged 17 years, of no occupation, living in Eyre Street Hill and her father was James McDonald, occupation tailor. They were married in Saint Peter's Italian Church as Roman Catholics. Martino was able to sign his name but Ellen could only make her mark. The witnesses were Benedette and Mary Alens both of whom signed with their mark.

1.7 Martino's first marriage to Ellen McDonald

Birth certificates in more detail

The top of the birth certificate gives the district name and this information is important when searching indexes. It is important to remember that boundaries were constantly changing, including not only counties but parishes. For instance, I knew that an ancestor died in Brixton but the registration district in the indexes is Lambeth. Also, villages in rural areas such as Devon could share the registration district of the nearest large town even though situated some distance away. This can be very misleading and it is always worth looking up registration districts in Genuki. (http://www.fhsc.org.uk/genuki/reg/)

First column on your birth certificate is the GRO reference

Numbered 1 to 500 the GRO reference is for a complete page in a register. Twins on the same page will have the same reference number, but if the twins were the last entry on one page and the first on the next they will have consecutive reference numbers. Another point to remember is that some families may have two births that appear as if they are twins when in fact they could be cousins or not even related.

Column 1 – date and place of birth

The date of birth is not always accurate, reasons include:

Parents were not above telling lies when registering a child outside the six week rule of registration.

Parents often became confused about the various dates of birth for their children as you will find on the Census where you sometimes find brothers' and sisters' ages switched in error.

The place of birth can be helpful during later registrations but in earlier ones you will find that in some instances only the name of the village is given, as with earlier Census.

When finding a full address a useful check is to see if the mother or father has registered the birth and given the same address as the place of birth for the child. It is important to remember some women went home to their mother's to give birth, but even if a child was born in an institution there could be a clue to the location of the family if the address of the informant is listed. If there is no address other than the institution then the area itself could be a clue or an old map might show the nearest institution to where the family resided although this could be many miles from the family home.

Column 2 – forenames/given name

The forename or names are in this column. A child can be registered without a first name due to the fact that the child died before registration, or because they do not as yet have a name, or because the child was abandoned, born into poverty or going to be adopted.

Where there are no father's details in the register you might be lucky enough to find two Christian names with the later proving to be the surname of the father.

Remember that a person might be registered with a given name, as with one of my ancestors Alice Amy Plummer, who was known as Amy throughout her life. Or perhaps they were known by a nickname bearing no resemblance to their given name.

Column 3 – sex

Mistakes have been made in recording the sex of the child when a name can be used for either sex, such as Francis and Frances, if spelt incorrectly. Or unusual names are given such as Asor Zoar, one of my ancestors, female incidentally. Another ancestor of mine Stephen had two baptism registrations – one for Stephen in FamilySearch.com and one for Stephanie in the National Burial Index. At first I thought they were twins as both were christened at the same time but further investigation at the original Church Records at the Surrey History Centre proved there was a mistake made in transcription in the National Burial Index and Stephanie was in fact Stephen. Always allow for human error!

Column 4 – father's name

At the beginning of Civil Registration, 1837, the rules of registration were open to interpretation. They stated that a birth should be registered within 42 days but it wasn't necessary to record the name of the fathers of bastard children. This meant that some registrars recorded the names of both parents even if not married and others only the mother if the parents were unmarried. This situation was clarified in the mid 1800s with clear instructions for registrars. It was stated that if parents were not married the father's name should be left blank. Towards the third quarter of the 19th century the fathers of illegitimate children could be added if both parents were in agreement.

Even when the name of the father is recorded on a birth certificate it is open to question when a couple are not married. This can also cause problems when no father is named on a birth certificate and this can carry on for generations.

My five times great grandfather, after the death of his first wife, became involved in a second relationship. So far no record of a marriage has been found. He inherited two children by the surname Webber. Neither child had the name of the father on their birth certificates, but I am aware this does not mean that Frederick was not the father of her earlier children. Both of her children used the name Pudvine and when the boy married he actually named his children Pudvine, when they should have been know as Webber, and the name Pudvine continues in that family to this day.

Column 5 – mother's name
Column 5 gives the name of the mother of the baby and will also include previous names if married. For instance, I found one birth certificate with the mother's married surname as Garbett, late Burnett formerly Clarke as she had been previously married.

In later records it is possible to find a mother registered with the name she has adopted, such as Brown, but it will also include otherwise Walker, although this is not always the case. My great grandmother Azor Zoar is shown on the birth certificates of her children as Azor Zoar Brown, formerly Walker, although she was never married to the father of her children. Again it is important to remember that, as with the stepson of my five times great grandfather, a female could also record herself formally by her step name.

Column 6 – father's occupation
This is the occupation of the father. Sometimes this can be blank, either because the informant did not know the occupation of the father, or the father was unemployed, i.e. not in paid employment. Sometimes the occupation may be listed as a labourer but there were many forms of labourers. My husband's great grandfather is recorded as being a carman on one birth certificate, an ice merchant on the next, then back to carman on the next.

Column 7 – signature, description and residence of the informant
Once the entry has been checked by the informant, he or she signs Column 7 with their usual signature. If the informant can't write they will

put their mark, usually an X, and the registrar will add 'the mark of…'.
When you see that the informant cannot write it probably means they
cannot read, so they are relying on the registrar to record everything
correctly to the best of his ability, which can cause problems. The first wife
of Martino Marelli, my husband's great grandfather, could not write and
one of her children was recorded as Ellen Morrelli and in my early days of
research this caused me great trouble. It is also worth remembering that a
signature is not always proof that they were literate. Many people learnt to
write their names but that was as far as their education went.

Informants can be the mother, the father if married to the mother, both
parents if not married to each other (this came into being in the last quarter
of the 1800s), someone present at the birth (grandparents, aunt, midwife,
etc), or the owner or occupier of a property or institution such as a master at
a workhouse, or a person with responsibility for a child, a relative or family
friend, or the master of an institution if the mother died in childbirth.

Addresses given can be misleading, especially if the mother goes to the
home of a friend or relative to have her child. You could also have the
address where born recorded the same as residence of informant if the
mother is registering the birth and think you have the correct address for
the family, but the mother might be recording her residence at the time
of the birth. Also, when someone else is registering the birth the address
will be that of the informant and the place of birth could be the address
where the child was born and not the family address, the address given
could also be many miles away from the true family residence.

Column 8 – date of registration

The date of registration is important as this will be the date recorded in
the indexes and not the date of birth. My own mother was born on 28
February 1929 but her birth was not registered until 16 April 1929, so
when searching for a copy of her birth certificate we found her not in the
March quarter but in the June quarter of the indexes.

If the child was not registered within the given period required by the law
it is possible the child was never registered, as with my husband's
maternal grandmother. Sometimes a birth is registered up to a year later
or longer if there was acceptable proof of birth from relatives, doctors,
etc. We must not forget a parent giving an incorrect date of birth in
order to escape paying penalties for late registrations.

Column 9 – signature of registrar

The registrar's signature is of little genealogical benefit, unless of course the registrar bears the same family name meaning there could be a family connection.

Column 10 – name given after initial registration

You might find a correction of the given name in this column if the name is changed at baptism. Usually a child would be baptised after Civil Registration, which could cause problems searching the indexes if the Christian name/s were changed and not corrected on the birth certificate.

Marriage certificates in more detail

Heading

This gives the place the marriage was solemnised, usually Church or Register Office, the Registration District or the Parish and the County. It is important to remember that the registration district will not always match the village or parish where the couple were living, especially in rural areas.

Directly beneath the details of the married couple you will be given more information about the religious denomination of the couple. For instance, Martino Marelli married Amy Plummer in 1891 at St George's Catholic Church according to the rites of the Roman Catholics. Some of their children have similar information but others have 'according to the rites of the Established Church' (the Church of England).

Entry Number

A church will have two identical registers and when they are complete one book is deposited with the superintendent registrar but the other is kept by the church authorities and may finish up in the county record office or in the local church.

Some 500 entry registers are as yet incomplete and it is quite possible that the information has never been passed to a superintendent registrar, so there is no record of the marriages in a church in their district. The GRO, however, takes this type of information quarterly, which is why you will often find a certificate via the GRO where you may have failed via your local registrar.

Column 1 – date of marriage.

A marriage entry is dated on the day a marriage took place. There are various ways of recording the dates of marriages as I found with the following:

27th April 1931
Sept 14th 1932
Twentieth January 1926
November 16 (with the year 1851 in the header)
May 1 1879

Column 2 – name & surname of bride and groom

It is important to remember that the name and surname of the bride and groom are not always as recorded on their birth certificates. Until later years they were not asked for proof of identity at the time of their marriage, just simply the names they were known as. Therefore, they could use different Christian names, as with Alice Amy Plummer who married using the name of Amy Plummer. Or my Henry George Webber who not only was known as George Henry on his marriage certificate but used the name of his stepfather rather than his birth name. Some people were known by aliases for many different reasons and hid their true identities, others for bigamous reasons.

Column 3 – age at the date of marriage

Again, the couple were not asked to prove their age or identity so these dates could vary enormously to the truth. Reasons might be they were under age, the bride might be older than her husband, or maybe they had to guess their ages as they did not have copies of the birth records. Also, if a couple stated they were 21 years or over they were not required to give their ages, and if they were in fact under age and married without the consent of their legal guardian the marriage itself could be classed as illegal.

I have a marriage record dated May 1 1879 with the ages of the couple simply recorded as 'full' and another as 'both of full age'. Interestingly, I have one ancestor Asor Zoar who had children previously from a relationship in which she was unmarried but went on to marry someone else in 1911 aged 28 years, but she records her age as 33 years, maybe because the man she married was 50 years of age, or maybe because she was confused.

Column 4 – condition

This column records the marital status of the persons getting married usually Spinster, Bachelor, Widow or Widower.

Of course we have to allow for the possibility that one or the other might be lying as they might record themselves as single because they are already married, or maybe they record themselves as a widow or widower when not actually married to the previous partner that they shared a home, life and children with.

If for some reason a previous marriage was annulled because of age or the marriage was never consummated or the female lied about being pregnant, they would revert to their previous condition and be recorded as single.

Divorce during the 19th century was a drawn out and expensive business forcing couples to either stay together but living separate lives, to move on into another relationship without marriage or to marry bigamously.

Column 5 – occupation

The next column shows the occupation of both parties at the time of their marriage. If left blank or if there is a line through this column it does not mean that the person concerned was not employed, especially if the marriage took place during the 19th century and the party concerned was female. Again, as with birth certificates, occupations could be embellished. One of my ancestors records himself as a provision dealer when he was a shop assistant.

Column 6 – residence at the time of Marriage

The address at the time of the marriage can often be a misleading column.

Couples would frequently marry away from the districts in which they lived for a variety of reasons. Maybe there was no suitable church where they resided, or perhaps there wasn't a church of the correct religion locally. Also we have to remember that one or both parties would have to establish residency in the location they wished to get married. Maybe they both went to stay with a relative, or maybe they both give the same address, although one might be living elsewhere. Maybe one or both parties did not have a static address and lied about their place of residence or gave that of a friend or relative in order to get married. Sometimes you will find only the village or street recorded as the address in earlier certificates, such as one I have for my three times great grandfather that records the address for both parties as simply Stoke (Guildford).

Column 7 and 8 – father's name, surname and rank or profession

These two columns relate to the fathers of the bride and groom.

The information in these columns should relate to the natural fathers of the couple in question but again the information can be misleading. My George Henry or Henry George Pudvine, although using the surname of his step father, does not record his father's details on his marriage certificate. There could be several reasons for this: he knew that Frederick Pudvine was not his father; maybe he'd lost touch with Frederick and believed him to be deceased; or of course that he was never told who his true father was. Legally he was required to add only the details of his natural father, but legally he wasn't really a Pudvine.

Sometimes couples chose not to record the names of their fathers for personal reasons and although these columns were to be used only for natural parents they were not obliged to fill in this information. However, I imagine that many fabricated details of fathers where none existed to save embarrassment. Martino Marelli was brought up in a foundlings home in Milan and his parents are recorded as unknown, yet on his first marriage certificate he records his father as Martino Marelli, a carman (identical to himself) but on his second marriage certificate he records his father as Angelo Marelli, a farmer. Was there any truth in this? Maybe he was told his father's name as a child in Milan. Maybe he fabricated a father as he was of the Catholic faith and to be illegitimate was a stigma.

If a father was deceased at the time of the marriage it was usually recorded as such under the name but not always.

The occupation is the last column and will give the occupation of the father, but if retired it will usually state that he is retired. Again, occupations are open to interpretation. For Martino I have his occupations listed on his children's marriage certificates as fishmonger, master fishmonger, shop keeper, tradesman and restaurant proprietor. I know that he was a carman, then ice merchant, then fishmonger and finally he owned a chain of fish and chip shops, so all of the descriptions are correct although different.

When relying on occupations to verify an ancestor it is wise to remember that some occupations had several descriptions but the meaning could be the same.

The line beginning with 'Married in'

After rites and ceremonies underneath the details of the couple married, the last part starting with the word 'by' and followed with 'by me' or 'after and by me' will have the following possibilities:

'by certificate' = found on a register office marriage and shows the couple gave three weeks' notice.

'by licence' = means the couple may have married under three weeks' notice. Maybe they needed to marry in a hurry or maybe there was another reason for the short notice, such as moving away.

'after banns' = Church of England marriage.

'by common licence' = Church of England marriage, meaning a licence has been granted by the Bishop of the diocese.

'by special licence' = Church of England. The licence here is issued by the Archbishop allowing a couple to marry in a church of their choice.

'by Registrar Generals' = found on any denomination except if a marriage was by the Church of England rites. Issued for special reasons allowing a couple to get married at any time or place due to the impending death of one of the party.

'by superintendent registrars certificate' = a Church of England marriage, but instead of banns being called in the church publicly notice of marriage has been given to the superintendent registrar. Reasons for this could include a need to keep the marriage private by the church or for the party in question. Having banns read out meant that anyone could view these records and create problems for the couple in question if perhaps one was of another religion or latterly if a couple was divorced.

The signatures at the bottom of the certificate

These signatures include those of the married couple and their witnesses. Although they are supposed to be signatures, their names are frequently written in full and do not give a true indication of a proper signature for verification purposes.

Generally witnesses should be personally known to the bride or groom, but again it is possible that the witnesses have been hired or pulled in from the street in some instances. Witnesses should be carefully scrutinised as more often than not they can be family members, married sisters, nieces or nephews, brothers or sisters, mothers, aunts and uncles. Usually there are two witnesses but sometimes you will find several witnesses on a certificate.

The last signature on the certificate is for the person or persons conducting the ceremony. Register Office marriages have two signatures, those of the superintendent conducting the ceremony and that of the Registrar who is doing the registration. The Church of England marriages have just the signature of the cleric in the main.

The certificate has the date the certificate was issued, same day usually.

If there are any corrections to be made on a marriage certificate you will find these in the space to the right of the certificate, otherwise you will find a line drawn through it. Although it is possible to find corrections have been added after a line was drawn through this space.

By analysing your documents thoroughly you begin to build evidence for future searches.

What the information we have this far tells us:

◆ Martino's marriage certificate gives an approximate date of birth for him of about 1852; this matched with the document from the Foundlings Home in Milan.

◆ Martino had been an ice merchant as Bert had told us but also a carman.

◆ Martino could at least write his name.

◆ Martino moved address often.

◆ Martino was Italian Catholic – this is strange as Brian is Church of England, as was Bert and his father before him.

1.8 Brian's Ancestors

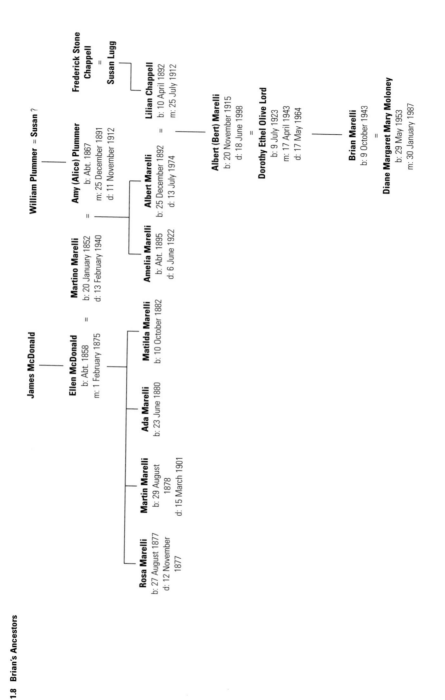

James McDonald

William Plummer = Susan ?

Ellen McDonald
b: Abt. 1858
m: 1 February 1875

=

Martino Marelli
b: 20 January 1852
d: 13 February 1940

=

Amy (Alice) Plummer
b: Abt. 1867
m: 25 December 1891
d: 11 November 1912

Frederick Stone
Chappell
=
Susan Lugg

Rosa Marelli
b: 27 August 1877
d: 12 November
1877

Martin Marelli
b: 29 August
1878
d: 15 March 1901

Ada Marelli
b: 23 June 1880

Matilda Marelli
b: 10 October 1882

Amelia Marelli
b: Abt. 1895
d: 6 June 1922

Albert Marelli
b: 25 December 1892
d: 13 July 1974

=

Lilian Chappell
b: 10 April 1892
m: 25 July 1912

Albert (Bert) Marelli
b: 20 November 1915
d: 18 June 1998

=

Dorothy Ethel Olive Lord
b: 9 July 1923
m: 17 April 1943
d: 17 May 1964

Brian Marelli
b: 9 October 1943

=

Diane Margaret Mary Moloney
b: 29 May 1953
m: 30 January 1987

◆ Martino had been married twice, first to Ellen and then to Amy. Being Catholic it is unlikely that he divorced, so his first wife most likely died.

◆ Martino has given two Christian names for his father, Martino and Angelino, yet he is a foundling. Did he know his father or was he perhaps embarrassed that he did not know his father and made up a name?

◆ John Fred Marelli appeared remote from Martino but we will have to dig further on him to be certain.

◆ Ellen Mc/MackDonald's birth is given as *circa* 1858 as she was 17 when she married Martino.

◆ The name of Ellen Mc/MackDonald's father is given as James and his occupation as a tailor.

◆ Rosa, Martino's daughter, who was born in 1877, is not mentioned on the Naturalisation certificate, so she is either living away from home or perhaps dead.

◆ The informant at Martino's death, M. Davies, could be his daughter Matilda.

◆ Brian and his sons Ian and Jason are descendants of Martino's second marriage to Amy.

◆ You can have spelling variations on records of the same surnames as with McDonald or MackDonald.

Already we are beginning to gain a fabulous insight into Martino's life and that of his family and Brian's family tree is growing rapidly as can be seen in figure 1.8.

	Mar	Jun	Sept	Dec		Mar	Jun	Sept	Dec		Mar	Jun	Sept	Dec		Mar	Jun	Sept	Dec
1866					1896					1926					1956				
1867					1897					1927					1957				
1868					1898					1928					1958				
1869					1899					1929					1959				
1870					1900					1930					1960				
1871					1901					1931					1961				
1872					1902					1932					1962				
1873					1903					1933					1963				
1874					1904					1934					1964				
1875					1905					1935					1965				
1876					1906					1936					1966				
1877					1907					1937					1967				
1878					1908					1938					1968				
1879					1909					1939					1969				
1880					1910					1940					1970				
1881					1911					1941					1971				
1882					1912					1942					1972				
1883					1913					1943					1973				
1884					1914					1944					1974				
1885					1915					1945					1975				
1886					1916					1946					1976				
1887					1917					1947					1977				
1888					1918					1948					1978				
1889					1919					1949					1979				
1890					1920					1950					1980				
1891					1921					1951					1981				
1892					1922					1952					1982				
1893					1923					1953					1983				
1894					1924					1954					1984				
1895					1925					1955					1985				

1.9 Form to keep track of investigations

Enthralled is how I would describe our feelings about having created a family tree – and not just from the information we had inherited from Bert but from our own efforts. The sense of achievement is astounding. We so wished we had done this prior to Bert's death – he would have been overjoyed.

How could I not go on at this point? What would be the harm of finding out just a few more details?

I realised that although Brian is very interested in the results of the research it is not something he is going to be passionate about. I on the other hand wanted to return to the FRC and decided to go again the very next morning, but first I devised the simple form shown in figure 1.9 to help me keep track of my investigations. This way I can tick each year as I search saving me from going over old ground and enabling me to plan future searches.

July 1998 continued...

I arrived at the FRC at opening time. First on the agenda is Helen or Ellen, daughter of Martino and Ellen, or any similar sounding Christian name born in either 1875 or 1876 as Martino and Ellen married in 1875 and Martin, their son, was born in 1877.

An aside I ordered the birth certificate of my father Charles Maloney born in 1888, 65 years before I was born in 1953. I wanted to check if the spelling of my birth surname, Moloney, is really different to my father's — it is — and also to have a copy for my own records.

Using my one-form system for births I could not find anything listed in 1875 or 1876 for Ellen or Helen Marelli. I considered the possibility that Ellen is the illegitimate daughter of Ellen so I searched the same years for Ellen Mc/Mack/Macdonald to be on the safe side but still could not find her. I decided to take my search backwards and look under Marelli and the variants for McDonald but it was not until 1871 in the last quarter that I found an Ellen Macdonald born in Islington. Could this be her? I knew this would have put the mother at about thirteen years of age at the time of her birth but as unlikely as this might be I decided to order the certificate – it was all I had to go on.

My next stop was marriage indexes as I needed to confirm or eliminate the possibility that John Fred Marelli of Macclesfield was related to Martino. The only way I could think of doing this was to find John Fred's parents' marriage certificate that in turn would give me the names of his parents and maybe a link to Martino. I also wanted to look for the marriage of Matilda Marelli to a Davies because the name M. Davies is a witness recorded on Martino's death certificate. I chose to work on Matilda's marriage from 1903, when she would have been 21 years old, to 1910 first, then if I could not find her to work backwards from 1903. *I had no reason for choosing this method, it was just how I felt at the time.* I found Matilda's marriage in the third quarter of 1908. I then estimated that as John Fred Marelli was born in 1879 his parents could have married reasonably within the ten years prior to him being born; I could always go back further, or forward, if required. I started from the year 1869 and found details of the marriage of his father George Joseph Marelli of Macclesfield in the last quarter of 1870.

From marriages I went to deaths to investigate the possibility that Rosa had died, as she is not mentioned on the naturalisation certificate. I plucked some years out of the air starting at 1880. I was shocked to find a death under the name of Amelia Marelli of Lambeth dated in the second quarter of 1886, *but Amelia is one year old on the Naturalisation certificate in 1897, so who was this?* I then found a death certificate for a Rosalier Marelli in the district of Lambeth, and assumed this to be the Rosa I was looking for. This is dated in the first quarter of 1888. Engulfed by a strange sense of grief I decided to continue looking through deaths for other Marelli family members but found nothing until 1901. This was for Martin Marelli, who had to be Martino's eldest son as his name is also on the naturalisation certificate. The district is listed as Wandsworth and the certificate dated in the first quarter of 1901.

I had not prepared myself for the way these discoveries would make me feel so I went outside for a cigarette and allowed the warm sunshine to diffuse the gloom that had come over me. I felt what I could only describe as grief for those who had died but also for Martino to have lost so many children. Upsetting as this was I went back to continue with my search for Marelli deaths. This was a bad idea as I was beginning to lose my concentration through mental fatigue but also because the area had become busy. It was not until I reached the second quarter of 1922 that I was to find another death. It was for Amelia Marelli again but this time from Wandsworth! *Two Amelia Marelli's – perhaps this one is another relative of Martino's.* I ordered all the certificates and headed home.

If you have trouble locating a birth, marriage or death it is wise to consider the variants in the spelling of the surname, as with Mc/Mack/MacDonald above, that you are researching. The accuracy of the information recorded on certificates depended on the spelling ability of the informant or registrar and errors were also made in the transcription of records into the registers.

When looking for a marriage where you have no date you might have to do a blanket search over a number of years. Or if you have a child's birth date of that marriage then you might want to search backwards for a chosen number of years and also forwards as they could have been married after the birth of their first born. You might have the death certificate of a person whose birth you are looking for giving you the age at death. From that you can then estimate an age at which they could have been married. I always estimate, to be safe, that the person you are searching for could reasonably have married at about 15 years of age and I go forwards from there.

How do you know you have the correct marriage certificate? If we look at John Fred's birth certificate it gives the name of his father as George Joseph! This could also be verified by looking in the registers for the marriage details of his mother, Mary

Worthington, as the mother's maiden name is usually given on the birth certificate, as it was given on John Fred's birth certificate. Mary Worthington's marriage details in the registers would also be located in the same quarter of the same year. (Each person of the same marriage has a separate index.) It is not unheard of to find that the mother's maiden name is recorded incorrectly or given as the same name as that of her husband's so do not be despondent if you cannot find the corresponding partner's marriage certificate – it does not necessarily mean that you have the wrong person.

Generally it is recommended to work backwards in family history, from parents to grandparents and great grandparents etc. However, researching family history is not always straightforward and you will encounter dead ends surprisingly early on in your research. Sometimes the only way to solve a problem is to work forwards, looking at descendants or sideways looking at siblings of a particular individual in the hope of finding further clues.

The certificates arrived within the week

The first certificate was for the birth of Ellen MacDonald (*sic*), who although registered in the indexes for 1871 was actually born in December 1870. This proved, not surprisingly because of the birth year, to be the wrong Ellen MacDonald. The father was a Frederick MacDonald, occupation lithographer, and I needed the father to be James McDonald, occupation tailor, as recorded on her marriage certificate.

The second was the marriage certificate for George Joseph Marelli, a draper who married Mary Worthington. His father is listed as Domonic (*sic*) Marelli, occupation agent. *I think now that this family of Marellis is no relation to my family of Marellis. Will hold onto the documents and maybe investigate further.* What I had to remember here is that although the Marelli surname was rare in England in the nineteenth century, and still is now, it is fairly common in Italy so I reasoned the chances of the two families being related, although not entirely impossible, are remote.

The second marriage certificate for Matilda Marelli, dated 5 August 1908, was the right one. Matilda aged 27 years married Thomas Morgan Davies aged 25 years, a boot retailer's manager. They were married in the Catholic Church of St Vincent of Paul, Battersea. Thomas gave an address in Wandsworth and Matilda Battersea, his father David Davies is a toplate worker journeyman and Martino's occupation was given as fishmonger master. Witnesses at the wedding were C. A. Davies and

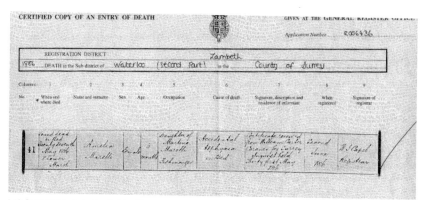

1.10 Death certificate for Amelia Marelli

1.11 Death certificate for Rosalier Marelli

1.12 Death certificate for Martin Marelli

R. J. Todd, but also Martino Marelli and Ellen Marelli. *Ellen is obviously the missing daughter I was trying to find. Ellen, Martino's first wife, had already, I assumed, died since he had remarried Amy by 1908.*

The first death was for Amelia Marelli dated 27 May 1886; she was only three months old (see figure 1.10). She was the daughter of Martino and Ellen and her occupation was given as daughter of Martino, a fishmonger. The cause of death shook me: accidental asphyxia in bed, and written underneath the date of death was 'found dead in bed'. There was an inquest because noted under informant was: 'Certificate received from William Caster, Coroner for Surrey, Inquest held 31 May 1886'. *Perhaps this was a cot death or perhaps the baby was in bed with the parents and accidentally suffocated?*

The second death was for Rosalier, another child of Martino and Ellen (see figure 1.11). Rosalier died on 3 March 1888, aged just three years, occupation noted as daughter of Martino an ice merchant. The cause of death was tubercular meningitis. The certificate also stated that Martino was in attendance. Rosalier died at home in Lambeth.

Rosalier and Amelia had such short lives but what felt more tragic to me is that they had been completely lost to the family. All that remains of those two little girls is two little pieces of paper.

The third death – for Martin Marelli aged 22 years – was dated 15 March 1901. He was also the child of Martino and Ellen. He died of 'phthisis pulmonalis exhaustion' (*sic*), basically meaning 'wasting disease, tuberculosis' (see figure 1.12). Martin also died at home in Battersea with Martino present at his death. What struck me as tragic here is Martin's occupation was also listed as fishmonger master, suggesting a father and son business.

The fourth death certificate was for the second daughter of Martino's called Amelia but from his second marriage to Amy. Amelia died at home in Battersea on 6 June 1922 aged 27 years, a spinster of no occupation, and daughter of Martino, a fishmonger master. Her cause of death was 'pulmonary phthisis and rheumatoid arthritis'. Matilda Davies from Brixton was present at her death. I wonder why Martino called two of his daughters by the same Christian name, especially as the first had died as a baby?

Now when I look at Martino's photograph (see figure 1.13) I see so much more than I did before – the pain behind his eyes, his strength and his pride. I can only admire this man who endured, with the evidence collected so far, the loss a daughter of three months, a daughter of three years, his eldest son at the age of 22 and another daughter aged 27 and most likely his first wife. Would they all have survived had they been born just a few decades later?

An aside The extra certificate was for my dad, Charles Maloney, and is dated 4 January 1888 (see figure 1.14). It shows he was the son of Charles Maloney, a marine stoker and Elizabeth Maloney, formerly Pilkington, living in Tatlock Street, Liverpool. *Dad is a Maloney but his children were registered as Moloney.*

What I learned:

1.13   Martino Marelli

- Sometimes births were registered late, as with the incorrect Ellen MacDonald.
- At some point in the future I would have to investigate more about inquests that might throw some more light on Amelia's death.
- Sudden/accidental death was investigated even all those years ago. I had such a false impression of Victorian life and family values – I thought they lived in the Dark Ages.
- I was learning medical terms and also medical history which got me thinking that when a doctor asks questions about the history of illness in the family how little we know.
- I was going to have to order at some point incorrect certificates, a risk worth taking if only to eliminate those nagging doubts or non-family members of the same name.
- It is worth doing blanket searches or one-name searches, otherwise I would never have found the forgotten children.
- Marriage certificates listing other family members can tell you that certain family are still living or still single at that time.
- Finding more of Martino's children and ordering their certificates has given me so much more information about some of the difficult times during his life, the areas he lived in and his occupations. I now feel I am beginning to get to know Martino on a personal level.

Death certificates in more detail

The top sections of a death certificate are the same as that of a birth certificate and, as with births, death certificates also have a GRO reference number in the first column between 1 and 500 and where two members of the same family are recorded on the same page they might have the same reference number.

Column 1 – when and where died
This is the actual date and place of death.

The place of death could be at home, place of work, hospital, institution or even in another district depending upon where the person was at this unfortunate time. So the residential address given here may not be that of the deceased but the address of the place at which they died.

The type of residence is not always shown in the address and although it does not state perhaps a workhouse or prison it is worth checking if the address was residential.

Column 2 – name and surname
The same care should be taken with death certificates as with birth and marriage. If a person dies alone they may be dependant on a neighbour to register the death and this person may not be in possession of the deceased's true identity. A baby dying at birth may not have any name, or just that of the father, or if illegitimate the mother.

Column 3 – sex
Although rare, some mistakes are made when filling in this information.

Column 4 - age
This is the age of the deceased at the time of death, although the age on death certificates, especially during the 19th century, is more often wrong than right, as I have found so many times when comparing birth, marriage and census records with deaths.

We have to remember that the informant of the death may be no relation to the deceased such as a neighbour or a workhouse master and be guessing their age. Also, the person who is deceased quite possibly may have been estimating their age due to lack of legal documentation. Even if family members are the informant they do not necessarily know the exact age of the deceased. It could also be likely that the deceased lied about their age for one reason or another, such as a female who was older than her husband. Even with children, mistakes can be made so it is advisable to seek further evidence for the ages of deceased ancestors.

Column 5 – occupation

Here the word occupation can have a different meaning to what we perceive occupation to mean. If the deceased is male, as with Martino, his occupation is shown as 'Fishmonger Retired' but the occupation of his wife Ellen was recorded as 'Wife of Martino Marelli Ice Merchant' and his daughter Rosalier as 'Daughter of Martino Marelli Ice Merchant'. Sometimes the working occupation of a female is listed as well as the details of the father, or it might say of no occupation if they were keeping house or ill, or sometimes even when they were actually employed.

A man could have no occupation shown, without explanation, meaning they were out of employment, or retired or perhaps ill. Also the occupation on a death certificate could be totally different to their actual life-long trade if perhaps in later years they became a night watchman.

If a child was illegitimate then their occupation would be recorded as daughter of the mother.

Column 6 – cause of death

Cause of death can be recorded as follows:

- ◆ Uncertified death – early recorded deaths where there is nothing other than the cause of death recorded, such as Old Age or Senile Decay. If the word certified is written under the cause of death is usually means a doctor has certified the death.
- ◆ Certification by a doctor – the most commonly recorded and usually with a doctor's name. (You can usually establish if a doctor has certified the death by the medical terms used).
- ◆ Certification by a post-mortem but without an inquest. Sometimes when a doctor has not certified a death or the cause of death is unknown a coroner may request a post-mortem.
- ◆ Certification following an inquest. An inquest is requested in suspicious or unusual circumstances, as with Martino's daughter Rosalier and once satisfied the death will be certified according to the circumstances. Rosalier's death is recorded as accidental but could have been recorded as natural causes. Sometimes it could read suicide or murder.

Column 7 – signature, description and residence of informant

The informant of the death would sign the certificate if able to write their name or they would make their mark as with other certificates.

The informant could be whoever was present at the death; this could sometimes mean a relative, even if the name is unfamiliar to you, or it could just be an unrelated neighbour, friend or occupier of the property in which they died such as a rooming house or workhouse. It is important to remember that earlier death certificates do not usually record the relationship of the informant or if they do it could record someone as being a daughter when they are really a step daughter.

By the last quarter of the 19th century more information about the informant is given making it easier to identify relationship to the deceased.

If a partner of the deceased is unmarried they cannot register the death unless they were in attendance when their loved one died.

When the informant is not related the information recorded is more likely to have errors, such as one of my ancestors being recorded as being the widow of her son Samuel rather than her husband William. Reasons for this could be that the informant never knew her father-in-law as he died many years before when she was a young woman, and that she assumed he had the same Christian name as Samuel, her husband.

The address or residence of the informant will be recorded much the same as recorded for births. Early records will more often record just a village, while later certificates will give a full address.

Column 8 – date of registration

Most deaths are registered within a day or two of the date of death but I found some deaths registered as long as eight days after the date of death. Reasons for delay could be because a person died in suspicious circumstances as with the death of one of Martino's children who died accidentally in bed and an inquest delays registration. It is important to remember that the date the death is registered is the date you will find it in the indexes.

Column 9 – registrar's signature

Here we have the registrar's signature but if a death is recorded more than a year after date of death the signature of the superintendent registrar is also required.

1.14 Birth certificate for Charles Maloney

2 Discovering the Census
(August to December 1998)

The evening before heading for the FRC I decided to go through all of Bert's paperwork again and to my amazement I found a handwritten scrap of paper listing some Marelli children including a Nellie, but not a Helen or Ellen, giving the birth date as 7 May 1876 (see figure 2.1). How did I miss this? Also listed are:

Ada born 23 June 1880
Matilda born 9 October 1882
Albert born 26 December 1892
Amelia born 28 August 1894
William born 10 April 1896
Amy born 8 February 1898
Kathleen born 11 December 1900
Winifred born 19 March 1902
Henry born 9 June 1903
Philomena born 11 May 1906

At the bottom of the note is written 'All Living' but Nellie, Ada, Matilda, Amelia, Winifred and Henry are all crossed through. So whoever wrote this note had obviously crossed out the names as they died. Sadly there is no date for when the note was written. Checking the signature of Martino on his naturalisation certificate and the writing of Albert, Brian's grandfather, on his National Insurance details of 20 May 1912, we ascertained that it was probably Brian's grandfather, Albert, who had written the information down. Albert died in 1974 and I knew that Amelia had died in 1922. As I had

2.1 List of living children of Martino Marelli found in Bert's papers searched the previous years I assumed the others must have died between these dates. I will now not only have to search birth details of the above but also deaths from 1922 to 1974 at some point.

Needless to say this is assuming that Albert did the crossing out on the list! Also I would have to search for Matilda under her married name of Davies and of course check that the others had not married, but first I would take the easy option and look under the Marelli name.

An aside: I phoned my mum, who was aware of my research, and told her I was going back up to the FRC and she mentioned that her mother, my nan, had never had a birth certificate. Naturally I found this quite unbelievable and thought that Mum must be mistaken but took the month and year of birth and said I would look it up if I had time.

For no apparent reason I began to feel unhappy with the search of deaths between 1901 and 1922 that I had carried out on my last trip to the FRC. I had been tired and might have missed something and it was preying on my mind. Call it instinct but I knew I would have to check these dates again. My gut feeling proved right for on my next visit to the FRC I found another Marelli death – this time, shockingly, for Amy Marelli, Martino's second wife, in 1912. What else would I find?

I continued with my search until 1922 but found no more Marelli deaths so would need to check under married names for those marriages I already knew about. Also, if I could not find any more Marelli deaths for the others after 1922 then I would have to search for further marriages.

It was then I thought about the earlier searches of Marelli deaths where I had started at the year 1880 looking for Rosa. Perhaps there were other children who had died. I decided to do a quick search from 1875, the year of Martino's marriage to Ellen McDonald. I found amazingly a Rosa in the last quarter of 1877, the same year as her birth. So the Rosalier I had already found is not the Rosa I thought she was. Time for another cigarette.

I felt depressed with searching deaths and although I had birth dates for several other of Martino's children these certificates were sure bets to find; I wanted more marriage certificates because they gave so much information. I chose to search from 1900 to 1920, using my marriage form, to look for the marriage certificates for Ada and possible marriage for Ellen/Nellie/Helen. I found only one during this period for Ada Marelli dated in the third quarter of 1902. *The marriages section was turning into a battle ground and although I wanted to search further I was beginning to lose my focus. I decided to look for Ellen Marelli's birth once more but I did not find her.*

An aside: I searched the final quarter of 1908 for my nan, Maggie Walker, but she wasn't there. Mum must have given me the wrong date.

Weary and perturbed I had to think of a way to find the elusive Ellen. Perhaps I should look in the Census for Martino? I headed upstairs and was given instructions for searching the Census. (Information on searching the Census is given later in this chapter.)

The only address I could remember was Homer Street. One of Martino's children from his first marriage was born at this address, so as he married in 1875 I chose to search the year 1881. It took me ages to grasp how to work the film viewer with it spinning this way and that, and I searched through endless incorrect places before it dawned on me I was not reading the reference on each section.

Finally I found Homer Street and started at the beginning, as I could not remember the house number. Unexpectedly on the second page I found a family of Plummers living at 6 Homer Street: William, aged 35 and head of family, was a railway signalman born in Tooting, his wife Susan aged 40 was born in Melksham and their children Henry aged four, Albert aged eight and Amy aged 13 were born in Lambeth. *What? Amy Plummer, Martino's second wife? This is not what I expected at all. My goodness, they must have been neighbours of Martino or is it possible they had lived at the same address?*

I searched frantically through the surrounding pages looking for Martino but could find nothing of him. I printed off the page and as it was getting late and as I was desperate to find the Marelli certificate with the Homer Street address on it, I headed home.

At home I searched through all the certificates I had and located the birth certificate for Matilda born in 1882 at 6 Homer Street, one year after the 1881 Census. *What did this mean?* Could Martino have known his second wife as a child and watched her grow up while married and bringing up his first family? Possibly Martino and William were friends? In 1881 Amy's father William is 35 years old, Martino was by then about 29 years old so it is feasible they could have been friends.

I was beginning to understand that families moved constantly either to better or larger accommodation as required or to find work. Maybe William had moved for some reason and recommended Homer Street to Martino, his friend. I started to imagine that Martino could have been having an affair with Amy while his first wife, Ellen, was alive but I still did not know when Ellen had died or if she had died, and quickly dismissed this idea as Amy was only 13 years old in 1881. I even considered the possibility that Martino could have been secretly in love with Amy while she was growing up, but hopefully this would have been when she was a little older.

Of course it could have been just a coincidence that both families had lived at the same address but I personally would like to believe they were friends and that, although Martino may have known Amy, nothing happened between them until after his first marriage was over one way or the other. Not that I wished Ellen dead or anything, I hasten to add – the last thing I want to do is upset Brian's ancestors especially as I am only just getting to know them. It is also interesting to note that the Plummers were not the only family living at 6 Homer Street. There were four other people living at the house, all listed as head of family, so it was most likely a lodging house.

The next certificates arrived:

The first was the marriage certificate for Ada who married Robert Johnson Todd – *I am sure that name is familiar to me* – dated 28 August 1902. Ada was 22 years of age with no occupation while Robert was 23 years of age with the occupation of electrician; both gave Martino's home address in Battersea. Robert's father was also called Robert and his occupation was given as bricklayer while Martino's occupation was given as fishmonger. The witnesses were Martino and an Ernest Williams. They were married at St Barnabas Church, Battersea.

The next was the death certificate for Amy Marelli, dated 11 November 1912. Amy died at home in Battersea aged 45 years, wife of Martino Marelli, a restaurant proprietor. The cause of death was given as phthisis pulmonalis haemorrhage. *How sad that he has now lost his second wife Amy aged only 45 – if Ellen died that is.*

With each trip to the FRC I am gathering more and more information and the family tree is expanding rapidly (see figure 2.2).

2.2 More of Brian's Ancestors

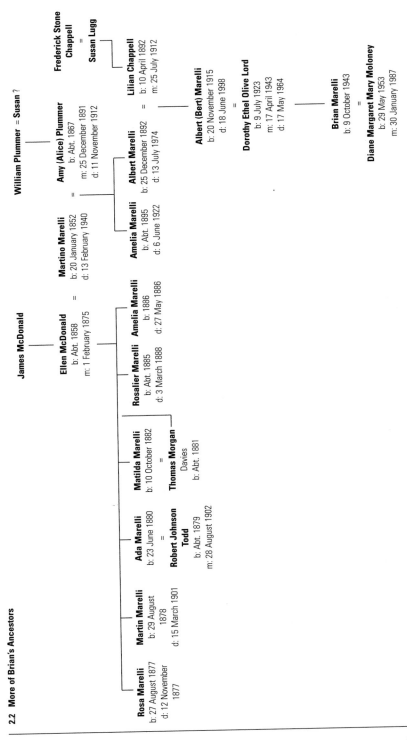

What I learned:

◆ Robert Todd, who was a witness at Matilda's wedding, married her sister Ada. A real sense of community and friendship is beginning to build in my mind for the children of Martino.

◆ There was a real possibility that Martino and William Plummer knew each other when Amy, Martino's second wife, was only a child. Maybe they were friends.

◆ In the nineteenth century premature death must have been expected and accepted. Did they view survival as a gift?

◆ That it was a good idea to go back over the documentation we inherited.

◆ The Census can provide links in your research that you could never hope to find on certificates alone, such as the Homer Street information.

◆ The Census also gives ages and places of birth of other family members.

Never throw away any documentation pertaining to family for what appears to be rubbish today could prove invaluable in family research tomorrow. Usually documents such as the ones we inherited from Bert come to us at a time of great sadness. My advice would be to deal only with the paperwork necessary to set affairs in order at this point and store whatever else you find until you are able to concentrate with a clear mind.

I called Brian's Uncle Vic and Aunt Betty who said that they thought Amy must have died relatively young as there is a family rumour that Ellen, Martino's eldest child from his first marriage, never married and chose to stay at home keeping house for Martino.

During August I went back to the FRC specifically to search the 1881 Census for Martino but could not find him. I also searched the 1871 Census for the addresses of Eyre Street Hill and Nelson Street, where Ellen and Martino where living at the time of their marriage in 1875 but could find nothing. Well actually that is not quite true because what I did discover is that the Eyre Street Hill area was known as the Italian Quarter of London and maybe this is why Martino moved there. I could not resist making copies of some of the pages from Eyre Street Hill because it was full of Italians with occupations such as musician, cream seller, ice cream seller and ice seller. There were pages and pages of them and it gave me a good feeling to know that although Martino was a foundling and probably came to England without a family, his countrymen at least surrounded him.

Next I looked at the 1891 Census for Martino who at this time was living at Lower Marsh, Lambeth. I found him! This gave me the impression of peeping through the window to a world that had long gone. Martino Marelli aged 37, head of family, is listed as a widower. *This meant that Ellen did die and it must have been between 1881 and 1891. How did I miss that on my search of deaths?* Martino's occupation was given as fish dealer and place of birth as Italy. Living in the house with Martino was Ellen his daughter aged 14, Martin his son aged 13, Ada his daughter aged 10 and Matilda his daughter aged 8, all scholars born in Lambeth. What was of great interest to me was that also living in the house were two Italian servants, Juilian Brofi aged 25 and Joseph Corfoni aged 24, both born in Italy and whose occupations were given as shopmen (*sic*). *I can only assume that they worked for Martino otherwise why would they be classed as servants living in his house? Martino had certainly come a long way in the sixteen years since his marriage to Ellen.*

The last person listed is George McDonald, the nephew of Martino, aged 16, occupation boot maker and born in St Lukes, London. *So even though Martino's first wife had died he still had her nephew staying with him.* What is interesting here is the possibility that by 1891 Martino was living in a large property with shop premises. Martino's immediate neighbours were two tailors and a boot maker, a boot shop manager, a coffee-house keeper and a chemist and druggist. *Further research would tell me that Lower Marsh was a community of shops with accommodation above and part of which still exists today.* Also on this page of the Census were people from Essex, Norfolk, Guernsey, Wiltshire, Cumberland, Somerset, London and Italy.

What I learned:

◆ You need a lot of patience searching through the Census if you do not have any leads to begin with, but you will get results if you persevere.

◆ The Census gives more insight into the lives of your ancestors, listing neighbours and their occupations, thus building a picture of the district they lived in and showing whether they lodged with others or were prosperous enough to rent their own property.

◆ London was as cosmopolitan in the nineteenth century as it is now.

- Despite the lack of modern-day transport our ancestors were able to and did travel extensively.
- The Census gives valuable information on who is living or deceased at the time the Census is taken. You can also source other family members or relatives lodging with your ancestral family.

The Census:

I admit that searching the Census on film or microfiche is not something I enjoy doing. I would far rather search online or on a CDROM but more about this later. The FRC has excellent information on 'How to Use the Census' on their website or actually on the first floor where the Census is housed at the FRC. There is also a team of helpful advisors at your disposal.

What is the Census? The Census is a Government survey aimed at gathering information on the UK population. The Census started in 1801 although only the information you will find from 1841 will be useful when researching your family history. For those without access to the Internet the following information will help you with your research. For those with access to the Internet then log onto www.familyrecord.gov.uk for an online guide to using the Census.

Information you will find on the **1841 Census**:

Christian or first name
Surname
Age (exact for those under 15 years if known, over 15 years the ages were rounded down to the nearest five)
Gender
Occupation
Place of birth (although for 1841 it was usually only if a person was born in the country of residence)
If disabled and nature of disability

Information you will find on the **1851 to 1901 Census**:

Christian or first name and Surname
Relationship to the head of household
Age and gender
Occupation
Marital status
Place of birth
If disabled and nature of disability

(There is a small amount of additional information on the Census for Scotland.)

Below you will find the dates that each Census was taken. This will prove helpful when looking for particular family members by birth date especially if they were born the same year for instance.

1841	–	**7 June**	**1851**	–	**30 March**
1861	–	**7 April**	**1871**	–	**2 April**
1881	–	**3 April**	**1891**	–	**5 April**
1901	–	**31 March**		

Census records have classification numbers for each year, these are very useful if you have lots of census information for which you have forgotten to write the year it applies to, see below:

1841	–	**HO107**	**1881**	–	**RG11**
1851	–	**HO107**	**1891**	–	**RG12**
1861	–	**RG9**	**1901**	–	**RG13**
1871	–	**RG10**			

Using the 1841 to 1891 Census returns

At the FRC there are surname indexes for some Census returns otherwise the minimum information you will need to search the Census, besides a name, on microfilm or fiche would be the district where your ancestor was living around the time a Census was taken. This information could be taken from birth, marriage and death certificates, family knowledge or other Census records for instance. Ideally you might have an address and may find that there is a street index available to locate the right film to view, as there is for some areas at the FRC. Failing that, if you only have an area/district then be prepared to spend many hours trawling through Census forms on microfilm or fiche.

If you are looking for someone by name then your first step will be to see if an index of surnames exists for the Census year you are researching. If there is an index you will be guided with further information. If there is no index listing surnames but you have the address of your ancestor you will need to look up a registration district, i.e. Lambeth, Epsom, Liverpool, etc. Once you have found your surname, street or registration district you will find the number of the microfilm you need to view along with a folio number that will help you find the area you wish to research.

When you have found the correct folio and page number – located on the top right-hand side of every second page on your film – write down this information. There are two very good reasons for this. You will need to locate the page again on another film viewer to take a photocopy or you may want to come back at a later date and review the page or the immediate neighbourhood. In addition, always write the page and folio number on any copies you take. A mistake I made was to take various copies from different Census years only to find once I had returned home that I could not remember which copy belonged to which Census year!

The above may seem complicated but remember that when you are ready to search the Census you will probably be better prepared than I was at my first attempt. Once you have mastered the film readers and microfiche you will find them similar to use in the various establishments you might visit during your research. Most places have excellent guides on how to research the Census returns and helpful staff available to get the novice started.

When searching the Census for ancestors where ages are known a useful tip is to record the age and address, if possible, of that particular individual around the time that a particular Census was taken. This information can be taken from certificates of the individual or their siblings as follows:

Name	1861	1871	1881	1891
Martino Marelli b. c.1852	Italy	Age c.19 years Living in London?	Age c.29 years Living in Homer St., or Oakley St. in Lambeth	Age c.39 years Living in Lower Marsh, Lambeth
Ada Marelli b. c.1880	N/A	N/A	Age c.1 year Living in Oakley St. Lambeth	Age c.11 years Living in Lower Marsh, Lambeth
Amy Plummer b. c.1868	N/A	Age c.3 years living in Lambeth	Age c.13 Living in Homer St., Lambeth	Age c.23 years living in Tooting

NB: Census returns 1841 to 1891 are now viewable free of charge online via Ancestry.com at the FRC. Census returns are also available on colour coded microfilm: 1841 Green, 1851 Red, 1861 Blue, 1871 Brown, 1881 Yellow and 1891 Black.

September/December 1998

From September to December I did not return to the FRC as I was battle weary but I did purchase a programme called Family Tree Maker. This is a computer package I had read about in the *Family Tree Magazine*. There are several computer packages available on the market, and each to their own, but I liked the look of FTM (Family Tree Maker) on which I could record a logical database of everything I had found, enabling me to link family members, record sources and build family trees. (A source can be a birth, marriage or death certificate, Census, baptism or christening record, etc., giving us proof of an ancestor's existence.) I had no idea how fulfilling the experience of logging all of my information would be and became obsessed with my new toy, but also frustrated when I realised how little information I had about my own family. It was then, while browsing one of the various family history magazines I had recently discovered are available at major newsagents, I read there is a site on the Internet called www.familysearch.org consisting of church records put together by the Church of Jesus Christ of Latter-Day Saints. (This is not a complete register of all church records and will only be useful if your ancestors were church-going people.) I spent weeks on this site, printing off various finds of some family names but not all. I added them to my FTM program at random until it dawned on me that I had no evidence that the Plummers, McDonalds and other names that my mother had given me like Cuffley, Reynolds and Walker, were genuine. It was a mess. I decided to scrap everything on my program. I started again adding only what I myself had researched or knew to be fact or had verified by viewing or obtaining copies of original documents.

What I learned:

◆ Information available via the Internet is amazing but should not be relied on completely and could be misleading if you do not verify finds with further evidence. *I now treat this information only as a clue until I check the record source personally.*
◆ There are monthly magazines providing you with not only interesting information about family history generally but also of other sources of research or guides and much more.
◆ To store your family information logically you will need a family history program such as Family Tree Maker.

Oh joy! I found, via one of the monthly family history magazines, that you could purchase the 1881 Census on CD-Rom, a must-have item in family research as far as I am concerned. The set of discs includes England, Scotland, Wales, the Channel Islands, the Isle of Man, the Royal Navy and a National Index listing everyone on the census by surname. (You can now view the 1881 Census free on the FamilySearch website.)

What fun and angst I had with this new addiction. Convinced I would find Martino I searched every known address I could find on the information I had but he was not there. I then tried variations on the spelling of Marelli, Marrelli, Marrello, Morelli, Morrelli, Morrello, Mirrilli, etc. It drove me to distraction and try as I might all of my efforts proved fruitless.

The 1881 Census comes with easily loaded software to view all the Census information. The information you will find on the 1881 Census are transcriptions of the actual Census which, although they are easy to read and search, does mean that you have to allow for transcription errors. The 1881 Census covers England, Scotland and Wales. You can search by name and locality and there is also a national index of names for the whole Census.

I did find possible members of my own family but at this point in time I was not particularly interested, as my family is not that exciting! Naturally I found William Plummer but I already had the original version from the FRC. I did find James McDonald aged 56 years, a tailer (*sic*), and his family living in St Lukes, London. This has to be Ellen's father but to be sure I searched other possibilities and was able to confirm that my first find was most likely to be the correct one. It listed James McDonald's children as Kate aged 11, George aged 7 *(George is listed on the 1891 Census as Martino's nephew but is actually his brother-in-law – it was further proof that I had the right family)* and Norah aged 2 months. Also lodging at the same address amusingly was a 48-year-old scavenger along with a 30 year old boot finisher and a 40-year-old bricklayer. The most frustrating thing was that James' wife was listed simply as Mrs McDonald, though it did give her age as 32 years so was this the second wife of James as she is too young to have been Ellen's mother? This would have made this wife of James McDonald approximately nine years of age at the time Ellen, Martino's first wife, was born.

Another find on the 1881 Census was the Chappell family from Lyme Regis. On the birth certificate of Brian's maternal grandmother, Lilian Chappell, it stated that Frederick Stone Chappell and Susan Chappell formerly Lugg, of Lyme in Dorset were Lilian's parents. The 1881 Census then provided me with the family of Fred T. Chappell *(the T must be a misprint)*. Frederick aged 30, occupation house painter his wife Susan Chappell, aged 28 born in Hawkchurch, Reginald his son, and an infant daughter aged one month with no name. *This last child was not*

Lilian as she was born about ten years later. Also living at the house was Frederick's mother, Mary Ann Chappell, a widow aged 68 from Axmouth, Devon. *How exciting, another generation!*

What I learned:

◆ The Census gave me a birth date for Ellen's father aged 56 in 1881, which meant that as he was born prior to 1837 when records of births, marriages and deaths began in England, if indeed he was English. So I would not be able to find his birth certificate but would be able to find his marriage certificate.
◆ James McDonald must have married twice as his wife is only aged 32 years on the Census for 1881 making her too young to have been Ellen's mother (Martino's first wife) unless her age is a misprint.
◆ I now had some of the siblings of Lilian Chappell, Brian's grandmother.
◆ I now had approximate birth dates for Frederick Chappell and Susan Lugg.
◆ Having such a wonderful tool as the 1881 Census on CD-Rom at home meant I could search at will with no time constraints.

Back I went onto the Internet searching for the names of Chappell and Lugg trying to find other family connections, but I did not have enough information. It did not help either making a stupid mistake like searching for the Christening of Mary Ann Chappell, as she obviously had married a Chappell and so therefore was not born a Chappell! This was a silly mistake I repeated several times with various female ancestors but I am still learning.

The 1881 Census was only the first of my purchases on CD-ROM. I acquired the National Burial Index for England and Wales, which although containing over 5 million records, is not comprehensive, and also the Vital Records Index for the British Isles, which again contains 5 million records of births, christenings and marriages from a partial collection of records in the British Isles but is not comprehensive. (CD sets like these of all types of family history archive are advertised in the family history magazines and some can be purchased from the Church of Jesus Christ of Latter-Day Saints, Distribution Centre, 399 Garretts Green Lane, Birmingham B33 0UH; tel: 0121 785 2200.)

It is more cost-effective to search the Census and find ancestors with approximate ages before looking for a certificate, but this could prove expensive in terms of time, especially if you have to search a whole county for instance.
The 1881 Census is viewable online for free at www.familysearch.org.

With my blood pumping I searched and searched my latest CD purchases but could find nothing of value. I remember cursing myself for wasting money on these items because they were useless but I was to learn that they would prove beneficial in time.

For the last couple of months of 1998 I stopped researching the Marelli family completely. I was at a dead end anyway unless I went back to the FRC. Also, as November and December are always fun, sociable months for us it was easy to allow family history to bury itself in the basement of my mind.

January came in with a bit of a yawn and I found myself looking to my computer to fill the socially drab winter nights and before I knew it I was back. Gathering together my forms for birth, marriage and death searches, I also devised another form to record the index information given in the registers at the FRC (see figure 2.3), this would also help me keep a record of what I had ordered. I had on one or two occasions, maybe a few more, not actually ticked the years I had checked either because I was randomly picking volumes on the off chance of finding something or because I was being a bit lazy. This was stupid of me because now I would probably be going over some of the same years again – but not any more hopefully. I made a resolution: I would become more organised.

Time and the 'people mania' at the FRC allowing, I was going to methodically check all the years for Marelli births, deaths and marriages and I was going start the following Saturday. And yes, I was going to get all those birth certificates for Martino's children that I already had birth dates for – about time you probably think but the easy ones, although still great to have, are never the ones you want.

Name		Cert.	Year	Quarter	District	Volume	Page

2.3 Form to record the index information given in the registers

On a Roll
(January to February 1999)

3

rriving at the FRC before they opened I was first in and began with marriages. Previous experience had taught me that within a couple of hours the marriages section would be heaving. I cannot stress enough how popular and dangerous this area can be for the weak hearted.

First on my agenda was a proper copy of Martino and Amy's marriage as I only had the extract. I found it straightaway in the December quarter of 1891 and noted down all the reference information I required on my new form. Next I thought I would search from 1898 to 1930. I found nothing until the last quarter of 1921 which was for Amy Marelli, daughter of Martino. The next was for William Marelli in the third quarter of 1924, the next for a Kathleen also in the third quarter but in 1925 and just when I thought it could not get any more exciting I found one for a Philomena in the first quarter of 1926. A gentleman facing me at this point looked across and raised his eyebrows as if to say, 'Some people have all the luck.' Marriages were becoming hectic as usual but so it seemed was everywhere else and I started to panic about getting all the births I required. So I grabbed some green forms for marriage certificates and decided to get those filled in while having a quick cigarette outside. What a pain it was filling in those forms and wasting valuable searching time! I decided there and then to take a pile of each type home with me and fill them in with all my personal details before I came back to the FRC again.

In births I first had another look for the mysterious eldest daughter of Martino, but as usual it was not there. I decided instead of just looking at the birth dates that I had for Martino's children I would do a blanket search starting from 1882, using my form to ensure I did not miss any others. I found Martino's second daughter called Amelia in the third quarter of 1894, William in the second quarter of 1896 – excellent! I now have his birth and marriage. Next is Amy, daughter not wife, in the first quarter of 1898; was I dreaming because I also had her marriage certificate? Then unbelievably I found Kathleen in the fourth quarter of 1899, Winifred in the first quarter of 1902, Henry in the second quarter of 1903 *(was Martino virile or what?)*, Philomena in the second quarter of 1906 and then a Hilda Marelli in the second quarter of 1912. *Hilda? I think Hilda is the sister of Bert!* I looked up from my research and saw the same gentleman from marriages facing me and smiled at him. He leaned towards me and said, 'I'm following you in the hope that your luck will rub off on me.'

My latest finds meant that I had four marriages to go with four of the children; I was ecstatic. I had already previously spent £104 on certificates and when you add on the train and taxi fare to and from the FRC *(I got fed up with catching two tubes and the walk each time)*, it was becoming expensive, so how could I justify spending another £84.50 on certificates? *Easily, I wanted them!* I went outside to fill in the rest of my forms when my mobile rang (you are not allowed to have mobiles switched on inside the FRC but I always switch it on when I pop outside). It was Brian to say we had been invited out for dinner that night so I could not be late. He also asked if I had found many certificates, 'not the one I wanted' I said, avoiding his question. I told him I was on my way home anyway because I was tired and could not find Ellen, the one certificate I really wanted. Brian actually sounded sorry for me and I felt guilty but also relieved that he had inadvertently stopped me researching further and spending more. Especially with the luck I was having, it could have been an extremely expensive day! *This was only the beginning of my fetish with certificates.*

The certificates arrived

Marriages
The first marriage certificate was for Martino and Amy and although I already had the extract I was so pleased I decided to order this certificate. It is dated 25 December 1891 and told me that Martino, aged 37 years, was a widower. It also stated that Martino was a fishmonger and his father was called Angelo Marelli, occupation farmer. Amy was a spinster with no occupation and 24 years of age. Her father was William Plummer,

3.1 (below) The wedding of Amy
Marelli to Joseph Evans in 1921

3.2 (right) Martino aged
approximately 69

3.3 (far right) William Marelli
during the First Worl War

occupation railway signalman. Witnesses at the marriage were W. Plummer
and E. Marelli. Martino was living in Lambeth at this time and Amy in
Tooting. They married at St George's Catholic Church, Southwark.

The second certificate was for Amy Marelli, Martino and Amy's daughter,
dated 9 October 1921. Amy was a spinster, occupation house-keeper of
Wandsworth, father Martino, occupation restaurant proprietor. Amy
married Joseph Evans, bachelor, occupation clerk, living in Stoke
Newington; his father was Francis Evans, occupation French polisher.
Witnesses at the wedding were W. Chas. Evans, R. Evans, K. Marelli, W.
Marelli and E. Marelli, I presume Katherine, William and Ellen Marelli
to be children of Martino. They were married at St Barnabas, Clapham
(see figures 3.1 and 3.2).

The third certificate was for William Marelli dated 6 September 1924,
aged 28, bachelor, of Lavender Hill, occupation engraver, father Martino,

occupation fishmonger (see figure 3.3). William married Winifred Edith House, a spinster of Battersea, Wandsworth, occupation shorthand typist; her father was Richard House, a builders' merchant. Witnesses were R. J. House and R Todd. They were married at St Ann's Parish Church.

The fourth certificate was for Kathleen Marelli dated 27 July 1925, aged 25, spinster, of Wandsworth occupation dressmaker, father Martino, occupation master fishmonger. Kathleen married Alfred Crawley aged 33, a bachelor living in Clapham Common, occupation messenger. His father was Alfred, occupation clerk. Witnesses were Harry Crawley, H. Marelli, W. Marelli, (H. and W. are Henry and William sons of Martino), P. Marelli (Philomena daughter of Martino) and A. Todd (Ada, daughter of Martino). They were married at St Barnabas in Clapham.

The fifth certificate was for Philomena Marelli dated 20 January 1926, aged 19 years, spinster of no occupation, living at Wandsworth, father Martino, a fishmonger. Philomena married Charles Hart aged 22, of Bromley, Kent, occupation a provision dealer's shop assistant. His father was Tom, a banker's night watchman. Witnesses at the marriage were M. Davies (Matilda) E. Brown and A. Todd. They were married at Wandsworth Registry Office.

Births
The certificates
- Amelia Marelli, dated 28 August 1894, daughter of Martino and Amy. *This is Martino's second daughter called Amelia.* Martino's occupation was given as ice merchant and they were living in Lambeth.

- William Marelli, dated 11 April 1896, son of Amy and Martino. Martino's occupation was given as fishmonger again, and they were living in Battersea (see figure 3.3).

- Amy Marelli, dated 10 February 1898, daughter of Amy and Martino. Martino's occupation was fishmonger, living in Battersea.

- Kathleen Marelli, dated 11 December 1900, daughter of Amy and Martino. Martino's occupation was given as ice merchant (master) again, living in Battersea.

- Winifred Marelli, dated 18 March 1902, daughter of Amy and Martino. His occupation was fish salesman, living in Battersea.

- Henry Marelli, dated 9 June 1903, son of Amy and Martino. His occupation was given as fish salesman, living in Battersea.

- Philomena Marelli, dated 11 May 1906, daughter of Amy and Martino. His occupation was fishmonger (master), living in Battersea.

- Hilda Marelli, dated 11 June 1912, granddaughter of Martino and Amy. Her father was Albert, the eldest son of Martino, occupation motor mechanic. Hilda's mother was Lilian Lucretia, née Chappell, living in Springfield, Wandsworth. (Albert and Lilian are Brian's grandparents.)

What I learned:

- I needed to take home a bundle of birth, marriage and death forms from the FRC and fill in my address details and basic information to save time on the day.
- That had I ordered the full marriage certificate for Martino and Amy I would have found out sooner that Martino was a widower and had been married before and that Amy was too young to be the mother of some of the children on Martino's Naturalisation certificate.
- That Brian's grandfather, Albert, did not marry Lilian until several weeks after the birth of their first child Hilda and that the address on both certificates is the same, so they were living together prior to the birth of their daughter and their marriage. Also that Albert, born a Catholic, brought his family up as Church of England.
- That when you have a rare name, such as Marelli, methodical searches over many years although a daunting task does bring results.

I wondered if any of the churches where Brian's ancestors were married still existed and one day 'on a whim' I searched the Internet for individual churches as noted on marriage certificates. I just typed in the church name and locations on the address line of my search engine i.e. St Mary's Newington, London and up they popped. Once again this extra, though basic, information helped me visualise Brian's ancestors. I also use this technique to search for ancestors on the Internet. Again simply type in the name of your ancestor i.e., Plummer family London, on the address line and you could be surprised with what comes up.

I made another short visit to the FRC to look at the 1881 Census for Martino, convinced that my CD-Rom version had somehow singled him out deliberately *(paranoia setting in!)*, and left him off but I could not find him on the original either. I also searched births again for Martino's eldest daughter Ellen but failed miserably here also.

In with the numerous photographs that Brian inherited from Bert was a photo of three of Martino's daughters believed to be Ada, Winifred and Philomena, with Martino's son's wife Lilian (see figure 3.4).

I now believed I had one or more certificates for all the children of Martino Marelli except for his eldest daughter Ellen from his marriage to Ellen McDonald and although the family tree was looking good, to me it was imperfect because Ellen was missing (see figure 3.5).

3.4 Left to right: Philomena, Lilian, Ada and Winifred

3.6 1881 British Cencus

1881 British Census

Dwelling: 1 Tyers St
Census Place: Lambeth, Surrey, England
Source: FHL Film 1341138   PRO Ref RG11   Piece 0596   Folio 132   Page 36

		Marr	Age	Sex	Birthplace
(Mr) MORILLI	Rel: Head Occ: Tea Merchant	M	28	M	Italy
H. MORILLI	Rel: Wife	M	23	F	St Luckes, Middlesex, England
H. MORILLI	Rel: Dau Occ: Scholar		5	F	St Luckes
Ada MORILLI	Rel: Dau		8 m	F	St Luckes
Martha MORILLI	Rel: Dau		3	F	Lambeth
Mary A. EVANS	Rel: Visitor		17	F	St Martins

Reprinted by permission. Copyright (C) (1999) by Intellectual Reserve, Inc.

3.5 Martino's wives and children minus the missing eldest daughter Ellen

Martino Marelli
b: 20 January 1852
d: 13 February 1940

Ellen McDonald
b: Abt. 1858
m: 1 February 1875

=

Amy (Alice) Plummer
b: Abt. 1867
m: 25 December 1891
d: 11 November 1912

=

Rosa Marelli
b: 27 August 1877
d: 12 November 1877

Martin Marelli
b: 29 August 1878
d: 15 March 1901

Ada Marelli
b: 23 June 1880
=
Robert Johnson
Todd
b: Abt. 1879
m: 28 August 1902

Matilda Marelli
b: 10 October 1882
=
**Thomas Morgan
Davies**
b: Abt. 1881
m: 5 August 1908

Rosalier Marelli
b: Abt. 1885
d: 3 March 1888

Amelia Marelli
b: 1886
d: 27 May 1886

Albert Marelli
b: 25 December 1892
d: 13 July 1974
=
Lilian Chappell
b: 10 April 1892
m: 25 July 1912

Amelia Marelli
b: Abt. 1895
d: 6 June 1922

William Marelli
b: 11 April 1896
=
**Winifred Edith
House**
b: Abt. 1902
m: 6 September 1924

Amy Marelli
b: 10 February 1898
=
**Joseph Sydney
Evans**
b: Abt. 1898
m: 9 October 1921

Kathleen Marelli
b: 11 December
1899
=
**Alfred Augustus
Crawley**
b: Abt. 1892
m: 27 July 1925

Winifred Marelli
b: 18 March 1902

Henry Marelli
b: 9 June 1903

Philomena Marelli
b: 11 May 1906
=
Charles Victor Hart
b: Abt. 1907
m: 20 January 1926

February 1999

One dull Sunday afternoon, nursing a hangover, I pulled up the National Index of the 1881 Census on my PC. I decided the only thing left to do in my efforts to find Martino was to drift through all the surnames beginning with M in the whole census then if no luck try the Ns and so on. *I was beginning to think that maybe Martino had gone back to Italy on holiday to get a tan or something and he somehow missed out on the Census but I could not give up without a thorough search and this, tediously, was the only way.*

What seemed like hours later I saw the name Mr Morilli and double clicked it with my mouse which told me to insert another disc – and there he was listed as Mr Morilli, aged 28, head of family, occupation tee merchant (ice merchant), place of birth Italy (see figure 3.6). The country of birth was right as was the age, but tee merchant? Next was listed H. Morilli *(Ellen)*, his wife, aged 23, place of birth St Luckes *(sic)*, *(St Lukes)*. His daughter came next – another H. Morilli *(Ellen)*, aged 5, born in St Luckes. Ada Morilli, daughter was next aged 8 months, followed by Martha, daughter *(this was Martin his son as Matilda had not been born)*, aged 3 years. Martino and family were living in Tyers Street, Lambeth. There was also a Mary A. Evans visiting, aged 17 years. *Evans is also a name that featured on Amy's, daughter of Amy and Martino, marriage certificate when she married Joseph Evans with several other Evanses as witnesses. So it could be possible that Martino knew the Evans family prior to his daughter's wedding and this visitor was a member of that family.*

I was thrilled to find this information but also frustrated by the amount of time it took to find it. Some reasons for this I suppose could be either that the person responsible for transcribing the information for the CD-ROM version had misread the original document as the Census is difficult to read, or that the enumerator was deaf and mistook Ellen for Helen and Martha for Martin if perhaps Martino still had an accent! Of course Martino's wife Ellen, who I believe was illiterate or semi-illiterate because she could not write her name, may have filled in the census form with the help of the enumerator *(who was deaf)*, so a bad combination all round. Or maybe Martino was still struggling with his English but I would have thought he would have known how to spell his children's names correctly. Anyway, I had found Martino and it felt just great but this information also gave me another idea! What if the birth of the missing Ellen, the daughter of Martino, was registered under the name of Morilli or something similar?

A trip back to the FRC and Births for the second quarter of 1876 saw me determined to find Ellen Marelli. It suddenly seemed so logical. *Why hadn't I thought of this before – I know better than this.* I started my search with the letters 'MO' and to my tearful delight there she was under the spelling of Morrelli. *Simple when you know how!* 'Ellen, I've found you', I said aloud, to the amusement of my fellow researchers. I did not need to explain myself because as I looked up the expressions on everyone's face told me they understood. I ran outside and phoned Brian and unable to contain myself I burst into tears. It was a truly fulfilling moment and a feeling of great relief – she had been getting to me and I did not know how much until I had found her.

Before going to family research centres such as the FRC write a list of possible spellings of your ancestors because once there and under pressure to find that elusive ancestor your mind does not function clearly.

I floated back inside to find the next ancestor on my agenda *(see I'm planning well now),* although had I gone home at that moment I would have been satisfied. It was to find the birth certificate of William Plummer born *circa* 1846, going by the information on the 1881 Census stating he was 35 years of age.

Having found Ellen I became the model researcher – polite, patient, smiling and perhaps a little bit smug as I was beginning to feel I was getting the hang of this. I decided to search for William Plummer in the years from 1845 to 1847 and found two possibilities. *This threw me right off my plan for the day to continue my blanket searches for Marelli ancestors.* One was for a William Henry Plummer born in Islington and one was for William Plummer born in Brixton. My dilemma was: do I order both certificates in the hope that one will be glaringly obvious and come back and do further research, or do I try and find further evidence like a marriage certificate? Before I knew it I was searching for William Plummer's marriage certificate from about the time he would have been18 years of age in 1864. I found a marriage for William Plummer dated in the last quarter of 1865 but how could I be sure it was the right one because I did not know the maiden name of his wife Susan and could not check to see if she was listed in the same quarter. I continued with my search looking for other possibilities until 1875 but there was nothing glaringly obvious so, a bit perplexed, I decided to order everything I had found so far.

I still had some time left, so did I go back to my original plan? No, I was now hooked on Martino's in-laws the Plummers, not in a warm caring way, but in a prickly, provoked way. I would solve this today. I went to look for the birth certificate for William and Susan's daughter Amy that would also give me her mother's maiden name. From my notes I was able to find details of the marriage certificate of Amy to Martino and knew her age to be 24 at the time of her marriage in 1891 and searched from 1866. I could not believe it – there were two possibilities again. One is for Alice Amy Plummer *(the actual name on her marriage certificate is Amy Alice)* born in Lambeth and one is for Amy Plummer born in Islington. *What is up with this family, why couldn't they pick original names and make this job just a little easier and less expensive?* Which one should I order... the Alice Amy, who should be Amy Alice, or the Amy who should also be Amy Alice? I instantly became my usual glowering self and ordered both!

Fed up with the Plummers I thought about going back to my original plan but the place was becoming far too busy and I had lost my rhythm. I went outside and filled in my forms having a well-earned cigarette when I began to wonder about Martino's first wife Ellen McDonald. Even though she was not strictly an ancestor of Brian's as he was descended from Martino's second marriage to Amy, she had still been a big part of Martino's life and I felt she should be recognised, so back I headed to Births.

From my notes I found the year of Martino's marriage to Ellen when she was 17 and that gave me the year 1857 to begin my search. I found several, one for 1858 in Stepney, one for 1859 in Hackney, one for 1860 in St George's in the East, one for 1867 also in St George's in the East and another for 1868 in Lambeth. The most obvious were the first three as they were in the right time zone. *Why couldn't there be just one, I wanted to scream. I couldn't order all of them!* I noted down all the references and stupidly decided to order the one for Hackney rather than look for further information. I needed to go home; I was tired and dirty from leafing through all those grimy well-thumbed volumes and a shower and a gin and tonic were beckoning.

An aside: I had a sister who died shortly after she was born. My mother has no record of her birth as my dad took care of things at the time, so I decided to order her birth certificate. She was born in 1958 but I also took down details of her death in December 1958.

The certificates arrived

My elation of the previous weekend was complete when I looked at the first birth certificate for Ellen Marelli (spelled Morrelli). It was definitely Ellen, born on 7 May 1876 as Albert Marelli had also recorded on the piece of paper listing all the Marelli children that I had found (see figure 2.1). The father's name was Martin Morrelli, occupation carman. *The spelling of Martino's Christian name did not bother me, because Ellen had registered the birth, signing with her mark.* The mother's name was Ellen Morrelli, formerly Mackdonald *(as previously spelt on other certificates).* They were living in the City Road area of Holborn. Of great interest was that Martino's first child was born in the 'lying in' hospital of London (see figures 3.7 and 3.8).

I had never heard of a 'lying in' hospital before so I went onto the Internet and on the address line I typed in the words 'lying in hospital London' and a host of sites appeared in which I found this website: www.hicksons.org. This site told me that the Lying In Hospital, Holborn, London was founded in 1749 for married women only. It was situated in Brownlow Street until 1849 when it move to Endell Street until closure in 1913. These hospitals were intended for the 'wives of poor industrious Tradesmen or distressed House-keepers' and the wives of soldiers and sailors. Anthony Hicksons built this website with a view to sharing Hicksons family information.

The next certificate was for the marriage of William Plummer dated 19 November 1865. *It was the right one.* William's occupation was given as porter but what convinced me most that I had the right certificate is that his wife was called Susan Jordan. Their ages were noted as both of full age. William's father, called John, was a painter *(not I think in the artistic way),* but it also noted that he was deceased. Susan's father was called Richard and his occupation was given as smith. They were married at the Parish Church of St Mary in Lambeth. Witnesses were J. L. Gawler and Edward Powell. Both William and Susan had the same address of Waterloo Road, Lambeth.

The next birth certificate was for one of the William Plummers born on 8 October 1846 in Islington. My heart sank – the father's name was William Plummer with the occupation 'coachman'.

CERTIFIED COPY OF AN ENTRY OF BIRTH — GIVEN AT THE GENERAL REGISTER OFFICE

[Birth certificate image — a Certified Copy of an Entry of Birth for the Registration District of Holborn, Sub-district of City Road, in the County of Middlesex]

3.7 The birth certificate for Ellen Marelli
3.8 Ellen Marelli aged about 45

The next certificate gave me hope but not certainty at first. It read William Plummer born on 1 January 1845 in Brixton. Father John Charitie Plummer, occupation builder. *This threw me, I needed it to be painter.* The mother was Hannah Plummer formerly Comfort. *William states on the 1881 Census that he is from Tooting.*

I looked at the next birth certificate for one of the Amy Plummers born in 1868, but the father was Horace Plummer. I quickly looked to the next birth certificate dated 17 September 1867 and there was Alice Amy Plummer, daughter of William and Susan Plummer *(not Amy Alice as on her marriage certificate – the naughty girl changing her name meant I could have missed her).* William's occupation was given as railway signalman. The certificate also gave Susan's maiden name as Jordan as per the marriage certificate, and their address was Lambeth.

The next birth certificate was for Ellen McDonald born in Hackney in 1859 and – *not altogether surprisingly* – it did not list her father as James McDonald, tailor – *another mistaken certificate.*

I was happy with my results although they weren't all correct and decided to check out William's place of birth on the 1881 Census – it was Tooting. I pulled out a map for London and established that Brixton is not far from Tooting. I felt more confident that I had found William's birth certificate.

An aside: The extra certificate: Birth of Kathleen Moloney dated 15th December 1958, daughter of Charles Moloney a Storekeeper Electric Cable Factory and Lilian Margaret Moloney formerly Reynolds. My little sister.

What I learned:

- Always check all variations of surnames when you cannot find someone where they should be – even make a list of possible spellings the night before embarking on your research.
- Sometimes our ancestors changed their Christian names later in life, much as people do today.
- Sometimes it is worth going off on a tangent, although it is easy to make mistakes.
- Even though you think you may have a correct certificate, as with the birth of William Plummer, you sometimes need further clarification such as whether a painter could be a builder or what districts are close together or perhaps have changed boundaries. (Information about boundaries is provided at the FRC and you can purchase maps defining registration districts.)

Between February 1999 and August 2000 I carried out no research at all due to ill-health but during a conversation one day with Brian's Uncle Vic and Aunt Betty I was told that Martino is buried in Brookwood Cemetery in Woking, only a few miles from where I live. The following Sunday afternoon, at a bit of a loose end, I persuaded Brian and Jason (Brian's youngest son, the eldest being Ian) to drive over to Brookwood to see if we could find Martino's grave. Brookwood is a large and amazing multicultural cemetery and we were fascinated as we drove around looking for the Catholic section as that is where Martino would be resting. We found the section fairly easily and started to walk down the rows of numerous graves when I saw Jason heading instinctively toward a large cross several rows away and momentarily got irritated as we needed to check all the graves methodically – until Jason called out to us. It was Martino's. We were stunned that Jason had singled out one grave in the whole area and it had been the right one. Again it was an emotional experience because not only did we find Martino but his eldest son Martin who had died in March 1901 nearly 40 years prior to Martino's death in 1940. Now here, generations later, stood Brian and his son Jason, 121 years after Martin was born and 147 years after Martino was born (see figure 3.9).

3.9 The grave of Martino Marelli and his son Martin

An aside: In April of this year I ordered the death certificate for my sister Kathleen. It is dated 17 December 1958, aged one day old. It did not mention my mother on the certificate but noted Charles Maloney as father. The cause of death was given as congenital implication, cyst in chest, attempted removal at operation.

Finding Martino's grave opened my mind once more to family research and I was again at my computer trying to pick up the threads of where I had left off. Sadly, although all my computer records and certificates were safe I had managed to lose some bits and pieces of information relating to previous research such as my blanket search forms for births, marriages and deaths. I was able to piece together some of the years but in doing this I discovered that in the years I had found a birth, marriage or death I did not complete any further research for other quarters in that same year. Something else occurred to me – my search forms had a combination of surnames against years searched. This was a big mistake, because how could I tell what years I had searched for which family? *I now hold a different form for every surname i.e. Marelli births, Marelli marriages, Plummer births, etc.*

An aside: In the course of another telephone conversation with my mum about Nan's birth certificate, Mum thought she could have been born a year before or later than 1908. This was feasible, I suppose, as Nan did not have a birth certificate.

Back on the Case
(October and November 2000)

A t the FRC, clear headed and ready for action, I decided to check for any other William Plummers or Ellen McDonalds but only discovered the same information I had already collected. I ordered one more possibility for William Plummer, just to put my mind at rest, and another for Ellen McDonald. I then did a blanket search for Marelli/Morelli deaths covering some old and some new years.

Interestingly I found a death certificate for Ellen Marelli, aged 30, in the final quarter of 1888. I was pleased with this find but annoyed with myself as I had already found a death in the first quarter of this year but stopped without checking further. *It took me some time to grasp that several members of one family can die in the same year, and, even if unlikely, it was not impossible to find two children born in the same year to the same parents. For that matter I suppose a person could marry twice in the same year. The only thing I am certain of is that a person can only die once in the same year!*

The next new death I found was for a Frances Marelli of London. I had only uncovered two Marelli families so far residing in England during the nineteenth Century and it intrigued me.

I hit a few dry decades and did not discover another death until 1966 for Harry Marelli in the registration district of Aldershot, the town where I actually work. This had to be Henry, son of Martino and Amy. The age given is 63 years which matched the year of his birth of 1903.

I came across another death, this time for a Stella Rose Diamond Morrelli and one for Anthony Morrelli. *Could they be more of Martino's children?*

The final death I discovered that day was for a William Marelli in 1977. This had to be Martino and Amy's son as the age again matched with the information I had for his birth. The place of death this time was Chichester. (A couple of years previously while away on a company jolly, I had visited the hospital concerned after falling from a horse and injuring my leg.)

From deaths I went back to births and did a quick blanket search over the years in which Martino and his wives may have had more children. Up until the death of his second wife Amy, there were none except for Rosalier in 1884 and Amelia in 1886. *Although I had their death certificates I decided to purchase their birth certificates to complete their history.* I was not really disappointed that there were no other children of Martino's *(15 is enough for any man!)*, as I now felt confident that I had found all the possible children and wives of Martino – it felt good, one mission accomplished.

An aside: I could not find Nan's birth details in 1907, 1908 or 1909. *Mum must be mistaken.* I phoned my Auntie Shirley and Uncle Harry – Uncle Harry is Mum's youngest brother – to ask if they had any copies of my grandparents' certificates and they sent me a copy of Grandad's birth and death certificates. Uncle Harry was also delighted when I told him I had been trying to find Nan's birth certificate because he had been trying for years but had been unsuccessful and now with health problems was finding it difficult to continue.

I also looked for the birth certificate for Susan Jordan, Amy Plummer's mother, from 1837 to 1847 but could not find it. Yet the 1881 Census states that Susan was 40 in 1881 making her date of birth *c.*1841.

The certificates arrived

The birth certificate I had purchased for Ellen Macdonald from the year 1858 was incorrect, as was the one for William Plummer in 1847. As disappointed as I was about Ellen I was now happy that I had the correct William Plummer in the certificate I had originally purchased.

The next two birth certificates for Amelia and Rosalier were correct, both giving Martino and Ellen as parents and both girls were born in Lambeth at the same address.

The three death certificates in the names of Frances Marelli, Stella and Anthony Morrelli were unrelated to Martino although Stella and Anthony were mother and son, and of interest, but of no value, is that Stella was the wife of a film actor.

The next death certificate for a Harry proved to be our Henry Marelli, and was dated 25 December 1966. The cause of death was given as coronary ischaemia (deficient blood to organ) and pulmonalis, cordis stenosis (narrowing of blood vessels) and atherosclerosis (hardening of arteries). Harry/Henry's occupation was given as fishmonger (retired) in Twickenham. (I met Henry's granddaughter while working for a company in Cranleigh. Both she and her mother would later come to our wedding.) Brian remembers visiting a fish and chip shop in the Richmond area when he was a child.

The next death certificate was for William Marelli, dated 17 January 1977 stating he was dead on arrival at St Richards Hospital, Chichester. It also stated his occupation as a retired camera technician and that he lived in Bognor Regis. His wife Winifred Marelli *(formerly House as per the marriage certificate)*, is named as the informant. The cause of death is given as myocardial infarction, coronary artery thrombosis, coronary artery atherosclerosis (hardening of the arteries) and cystic left kidney. There was a post-mortem without an inquest.

Finally was the death certificate for Ellen Marelli, aged 30, dated 4 November 1888, the same year Martino had lost his daughter Rosalier. The occupation for Martino is ice merchant. Martino was present at her death at home in Lambeth and the cause of death is given as phthisis – 12 months.

With all my recent finds at the FRC I was beginning to wonder how I would ever be able to print all of Brian's ancestors onto one page. I could not, so I have printed a tree of Brian's direct ancestors (see figure 4.1)

An aside: Copies of certificates for Granddad came in the post. Harry Reynolds was born in 1901 in Epsom, son of Robert Reynolds and Eliza Reynolds, formerly Cuffley. Harry Reynolds died on 9 May 1970 in Chester. *I was pleased with this information, although it did feel morbid to have requested Grandad's death certificate, because one day I might delve deeper into my own family.*

4.1 Direct ancestors of Brian Marelli

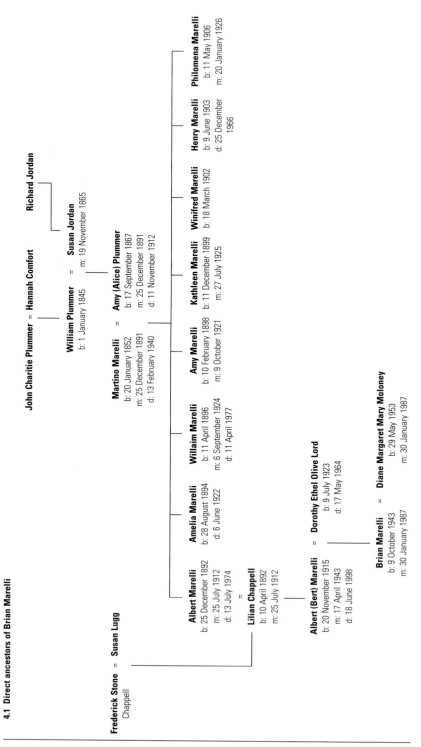

What I learned:

◆ Martino's sons both died of heart conditions.

◆ I was learning more about medical terms and the medical history of Brian's family.

◆ Even though I had purchased certificates for unrelated persons I still found them interesting and gave them due respect. I will hold onto these as you can never be sure that at some point in the future I may find a connection or even do a one-name study, a new term I had come across while surfing the net. Basically it means collecting the details of everyone with the same surname in a particular area, county, country etc.

During October and November I continued to make visits to the FRC and with each visit I started to spend a little more time looking for the birth certificate of my grandmother, Maggie Walker, without success.

I did order one more incorrect certificate for Ellen McDonald. The one I had looked correct except it meant she would have been only 14 or nearly 15 years of age when she married Martino *(unlikely to be right then)*.

The certificate for Ellen McDonald read: Ellen McDonald, born 1 November 1860 in St George's in the East, father James McDonald, occupation shoemaker, and mother Ellen McDonald, formerly Cockran. Looking back on the previous information I had for Ellen's father, James, on the 1881 Census I now believe that Ellen's mother's age is a misprint as Ellen's mother's name on the birth certificate is also Ellen. It also states on the 1881 Census that Ellen's brother was a boot-maker, like his father. This is more evidence pointing to this being Ellen McDonald, but I'm still not one hundred per cent on this. This also means that Ellen was only just nearly 15 years of age when she married Martino and not 17 (See figure 4.2).

4.2 1881 British Census

4.3 Marriage certificate for Frederick Stone Chappell

I hate to admit I also ordered one more possible certificate for a William Plummer I found who was born in 1849. This proved to be incorrect, the final verification that I did indeed have his correct birth certificate *(expensive but worth it)*. The need to verify records is of great importance to me – to most people I expect, as who would want an inaccurate family history!

This was when I took an interest in Brian's grandmother and Bert's mother Lilian Chappell and four further visits to the FRC during December brought me the following information.

The first time was a marriage certificate for Frederick Stone Chappell aged 25, father of Lilian, to Susan Lugg aged 24, dated 31 January 1877. Frederick's occupation is given as painter. *I was thrilled with this occupation because it cleared up my earlier query regarding the occupation of John Charitie Plummer whose occupations were given as both painter and builder.* Both Susan and Frederick were residing in Lyme Regis at the time of their wedding. Samuel Chappell, a shoemaker, is Frederick's father and Andrew Lugg, a farmer, is Susan's father. Witnesses at the wedding were Elizabeth and John Pitfield (see figure 4.3)

Further searching at home on the 1881 Census found Andrew Lugg, a Farmer, and his wife Caroline, living in Whitchurch, Dorset (see figure 4.4). Also residing at the house are Edward Lugg aged 20, Edwin Lugg aged 16, George Holman aged 15, Caroline Holman aged 12, Mary Ann Holman aged 11 and Ruth Lugg, mother, aged 87, a widow. *So I had now gone back another generation and, after the experience with Martino, I*

suspected that Andrew had
been married twice because of
the other children listed as
sons and daughters but with
the surname Holman.

Back on the Internet, the
'FamilySearch' site brought
me the marriage of Samuel
Chapple (*sic*) to Mary Anne
(*sic*) Sampson in 1836, in
Axmouth, Devon – *I love this
site*. This had to be
Frederick's parents because I
had a Mary Ann living with
Frederick on the 1881 Census
(where he is listed as Frederick
(T) Chappell, convincing me
the T was an error) and
stating she was born in
Axmouth (See figure 4.5).

4.4 (top) 1881 British Census, 4.5 (above) Individual record

I acquired the death certificate for Mary Ann Chappell dated 10th March
1893. *This is Mary Ann Chappell from the 1881 Census living with her
son Frederick Chappell.* The certificate states that Mary Ann is the
widow of Samuel Chappell, a shoemaker, Frederick Chappell, her son,
being present at the death. The cause of death is given as chronic
bronchitis and cardiac failure (see figures 4.6, to 4.9).

4.6 Death certificate for Mary Ann Chappell, née Sampson

1881 British Census

Dwelling: Pickle Square
Census Place: Lyme Regis, Dorset, England
Source: FHL Film 1341513   PRO Ref RG11   Piece 2126   Folio 70   Page 41

	Marr	Age	Sex	Birthplace
Fred T. CHAPPELL	M	30	M	**Lyme Regis, Dorset, England**
Rel: Head				
Occ: House Painter				
Susan CHAPPELL	M	28	F	Hawkchurch, Dorset, England
Rel: Wife				
Occ: House Painter Wife				
Reginald CHAPPELL		3	M	Lyme Regis Dorset, England
Rel: Son				
Infant CHAPPELL		1 m	F	Lyme Regis Dorset, England
Rel: Daur				
Mary Ann CHAPPELL	W	68	F	Axmouth, Devon, England
Rel: Mother				

4.7 (above left) Susan Chappell, nee Lugg

4.8 (above right) Samual Chappell

4.9 (left) 1881 British Census

CERTIFIED COPY OF AN ENTRY OF BIRTH

GIVEN AT THE GENERAL REGISTER OFFICE

Application Number W005506

REGISTRATION DISTRICT Axminster

1851   BIRTH in the Sub-district of Lyme   in the   Counties of Devon and Dorset

Columns:	1	2	3	4	5	6	7	8	9	10
No.	When and where born	Name, if any	Sex	Name and surname of father	Name, surname and maiden surname of mother	Occupation of father	Signature, description and residence of informant	When registered	Signature of registrar	Name entered after registration
102	Eighteenth Augustus 1851 Broadfield Lyme	Frederic Charles	Boy	James Stone	Selina Stone formerly Tuttule	Postmaster	James Stone father Broad Mead Lyme	Twelvemonth December 1851	Edw. d. Charles Kepenhar.	

4.10 Birth certificate for Frederic Charles Stone

I also acquired a marriage certificate for Andrew Lugg, dated 12 February 1852, to a Hannah Holman. The certificate gives Andrew's occupation as a farmer, and his father's name as John Lugg, also a farmer. Hannah's father is James Holman, a farmer, and witnesses were James and Susannah Holman. The address of Andrew is given as Whitchurch, Devon.

I had no luck in my search for the birth certificate of Frederick Chappell but I did find something very strange. Frederick's name on other documents is Frederick Stone Chappell with an approximate birth date of *circa* 1852, and while searching for Chappells I also looked at the surname of Stone. I found a Frederic Charles Stone, son of James and Selina Stone, formerly White, of Broad Street, Lyme Regis (see figure 4.10). I have subsequently searched and searched for Frederick Stone Chappell's birth certificate and keep coming back to this one. Did the Chappells adopt him? If so then Brian's ancestors are not who we think they are, but until I get to the bottom of this I shall leave things as they are. At some point in the future I must investigate James and Selina Stone. Goodness, so much to do and so little time!

I also found Susan Lugg's birth certificate dated 27 December 1852. It stated she was the daughter of Andrew Lugg, a dairyman, and Hannah Lugg, formerly Holman.

Last but not least I found a second marriage certificate for Andrew Lugg, solving my earlier query on the 1881 Census. On 14 November 1872 Andrew Lugg, a widower aged 42, married Caroline Holman, a widow aged 47. The certificate states that John Lugg, a farmer, was Andrew's father and Robert Spiller, a yeoman, was Caroline's father. *This is very confusing and took a little working out but I deduced that obviously Hannah was a true Holman, but Caroline must have been married to Hannah's brother because her father was a Spiller not a Holman, if you get my drift. So after Hannah's death Andrew married his sister-in-law, Caroline, whose husband had also died but whose father is called Robert Spiller!*

With the added information I searched FamilySearch again and found the following:

- the marriage details for John Lugg to Ruth Willey on 24 April 1823 in Axmouth, Devon;
- the christening details for Ruth Willey (spelt Williy) dated 24 May 1795, in Upottery, Devon, parents Richard Williy and Jane;
- the christening details for Hannah Holman dated 25 April 1830 in Musbury, Devon, parents James and Sarah Holman;
- the christening details for Mary Anne Sampson dated 8 May 1814 in Axmouth, Devon parents John and Elizabeth Sampson;
- the christening details for John Sampson dated about 1782 of Axmouth, Devon.

If you are confused by all of the above I will try and put my findings in context for you listing only direct ancestors.

Starting with Brian's sons we now have eight generations:

1. Brian's sons, Ian and Jason Marelli.
2. Their father, Brian Marelli.
3. Their grandparents, Albert William Marelli and Dorothy Lord.
4. Their great grandparents, Albert Marelli and Lilian Chappell.
5. Their G.G. grandparents, Martino Marelli and Amy Plummer and Frederick Stone Chappell and Susan Lugg.
6. Their G.G.G. Grandparents, William Plummer and Susan Jordan on Amy Plummer's side of the family. Also Samuel Chappell and Mary Ann Sampson and Andrew Lugg and Hannah Holman on Frederick Chappell and Susan Lugg's side of the family.
7. Their G.G.G.G. Grandparents, John and Elizabeth Sampson parents of Mary Ann Sampson; John Lugg and Ruth Williy parents of Andrew Lugg and James and Sarah Holman parents of Hannah Holman.
8. Their G.G.G.G.G. Grandparents, Richard and Jane Williy born around 1775.

As yet I have not found details of Caroline's first marriage to a Holman.

Tips for searching on FamilySearch

For the purpose of this exercise we are going to source the birth and marriage details for Mary Anne Chappell, née Sampson. She was approximately 68 years of age on the 1881 Census.

1. On the Home Page with your mouse click the box marked search. (When you go into FamilySearch you will find research tips on the Home Page.)

2. We are lucky because we have her full name and that will give us greater flexibility in our search than a surname only. For now we are only going to key in her first name Mary and surname Sampson. So type in Mary Sampson. (The reason for this is we do not want to eliminate possibilities and we are going to refine our research accordingly.) As you will see there are hundreds of Mary Sampsons in various databases such as the Ancestral File, US 1880 Census, British Isles 1881 Census, British Isles International Genealogical Index (IGI) and the Pedigree Resources. We are looking for birth and marriage details so click your mouse on the IGI Index.

3. A list of Mary Sampsons appears and you will see that there are hundreds of them, so to reduce this list we are going to go to the second page where we can refine our search. Click your mouse on the blue line at the bottom of the IGI Index that reads 'matches of IGI over 25'. You will now be taken into the complete listing of Mary Sampsons.

4. We could spend hours going through all the listings but if we refine our search at this point it will speed the process up. At the top right of this page click the blue line that reads 'refine search'. You will now be taken back into a more flexible searching facility.

5. As I only have an approximate year of Mary Anne's birth and because I also want to search for her marriage to Samuel Chappell (information taken from Frederick Chappell's marriage certificate) I am only going to put in her place of birth taken from the 1881 Census which is Devon. Select the county of Devon and click search with your mouse. There are now only 170 records to choose from. I could now go down the list looking for Mary Annes born in Axmouth and Mary Annes married in Axmouth or the surrounding area, or I could refine my search again by selecting the event of birth and putting in a year range and year for her birth.

6. Go back into 'refine search'. Choose the event birth and put in your chosen year of birth $c.$1813 in this case, as she was $c.$68 years in 1881, with a range of five years and click search with your mouse. As you will see the list is now reduced to 12 records and Mary Anne Sampson is easy to find.

7. Click the name Mary Anne Sampson with your mouse and you will be taken into the record that will give you more information and the names of her parents. (You can highlight her record and print the selected text or you can print the whole page.) At this point you can also click on the individual names of her parents or the blue line 'family' or 'pedigree', if there is one, that could also provide additional information. In my case there is no further information. So I am now going to search for her marriage.

8. When you have printed out or looked at the birth information click the back arrow on top left of the page with your mouse to take you back to your refined search page. We are going to change the event of birth to marriage and choose a selected year and range of years. In this case, as I do not have a date, I am going to choose an age when she would have been about 22 years old in 1826 and a range of 10 years. It is easy enough to spot Mary Anne's marriage in 1836, as there are only 16 records to choose from. I know I have found the correct marriage because her record states she married Samuel Chapple (different spelling of surname but the Christian name is correct) as per Frederick Chappell's marriage certificate stating his father is called Samuel Chappell; also, the marriage took place in Axmouth. Again a quick look at the families for both Mary Anne and Samuel does not give me any further clues.

At this point I can now go back to my 'refine search' page and look for the birth details of Samuel Chapple or look for details of Mary Anne Sampson's parents.

Another useful search tip for finding children of your ancestors using FamilySearch is this:
- find an ancestor that you know has married;
- refine your search;

Take out the first names where it indicates First Name and Last Name and put in the Father's name in full, and just the first name of his wife – you can leave in County etc and click find. You should now have all children born to anyone by the male name who was married to someone with a Christian name as that of your chosen ancestor.

Brian's family tree is becoming quite comprehensive although there is still a lot of research to be carried out and christening and church marriage records to be sourced. As you will see, the further back you go the more direct ancestors you have with each generation - 2 grandparents become 4, then 8, then 16, then 32 and so on (see figure 4.11)

What I learned:

- It is possible our ancestors were not sure of their age or date of birth or lied about their age for some reason.
- Ordering an incorrect certificate does help confirm you have a correct certificate such as with William Plummer.
- An occupation can have different titles such as painter and builder but mean the same thing.
- I would constantly revisit the Census as more evidence came to light.
- The further back in my research I went the harder it would become and I would have to find other sources of information such as Parish Records.

4.11 Direct ancestors of Brian Marelli

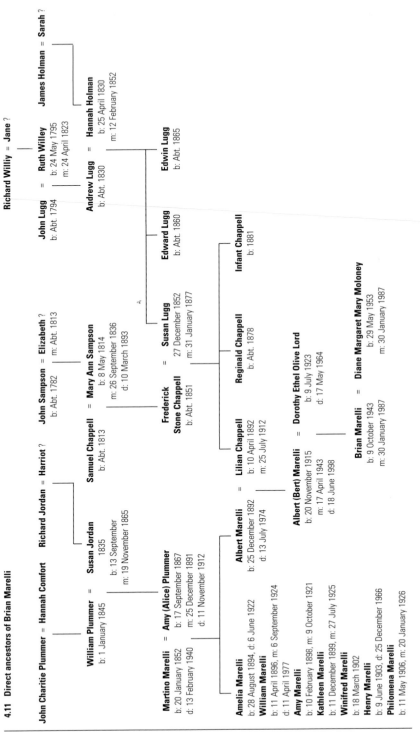

- Sometimes when you cannot find a certificate it is worth considering secondary names such as Stone, as with Frederick T Stone Chappell, which gave me a possible birth for him under the surname of Stone.
- It is possible for an ancestor to marry two people of the same surname as did Andrew Lugg, who married not a sister, but a sister-in-law.

A shift to my family

My youngest brother Jim had inherited, I found out, a good part of his family history on his father's, my stepfather Gareth Hughes', side of the family but wanted to know his maternal side of the family as much as my brothers Michael and Kevin wanted to know Dad's history. It was becoming evident to me that naturally the females in my family were mostly interested in our maternal ancestors while the guys were more interested in our paternal history – logical really. Feeling guilty that I had not found anything of interest on my side of the family I thought I would look for a death certificate of either my Grandmother or Grandfather on my father's side of the family. I found one for an Elizabeth Maloney of Liverpool who died in 1940; it was the wrong one.

On one of my visits during the month of November my mum and dad, my stepfather, came with me. As Mum did not have a full birth certificate we decided to look her up for a bit of fun and we looked in the first quarter of 1929 but she was not there. Initially Mum was upset because not only had we failed to find her mother, Maggie, now we could not find Mum, although I assured her that her birth certificate must exist as Mum had a short version, so we looked in the next quarter and found it. Dated 28 February 1929, registered in April 1929, it stated Mum, Lilian, is the daughter of Harry William Reynolds and Maggie Reynolds, formerly Walker, and was born in Redhill Maternity Home. What is of interest is that Maggie had to sign a declaration stating, we assume, that she was who she said she was.

We also acquired Maggie's marriage certificate dated 1928. Granddad's occupation is given as general labourer aged 27 years and Nan is a factory hand in a silk factory, aged 21 years. *This meant she had to have been born in 1907 or lied about her age to get married.* Harry lists his father as Robert Reynolds, deceased, a railway shedman (*sic*). Nan does not list her father.

4.12 Marriage certificate for Robert and Eliza Cuffley

4.13 Marriage certificate for Charles Maloney and Elizabeth Pilkington

Granddad's address is Surbiton and Nan's is Epsom. Witnesses at the wedding are Amelia May Loughby and Ada Louisa Reynolds. Could Amelia be a married relative and perhaps Ada a sister or sister-in-law of Grandad's?

We also found Harry's parents' marriage certificate, Mum's grandparents on her father's side (see figure 4.12). Dated 7th April 1890 for Robert Reynolds, aged 29, a bachelor occupation labourer, father unknown and Eliza Cuffley, aged 28, a spinster with no occupation, father Frederick Cuffley a labourer. Witnesses at the wedding were E Cuffley and Ada Sanders. *I wonder when a father is noted as unknown on a marriage certificate, as in Robert's case, does it mean that he doesn't know who his father is or does it mean he doesn't want to know? And how weird if Robert really doesn't know who his father is and then I, all these years later, might discover his father's identity.*

There was one other marriage certificate for a Frederick Reynolds of Epsom in 1880 that we ordered and also one for the possible marriage of my father's parents but both were incorrect. A further search though did eventually find my grandparents' marriage certificate on Dad's side, dated 13 February 1882 for Charles Maloney, aged 19, a bachelor, occupation wheelwright, father Charles Maloney a labourer (see figure 4.13). He married Elizabeth Pilkington, aged 20, a spinster with no occupation, father Robert Pilkington a labourer. The witnesses were Robert Hughes and Esther Jolinston.

We located death certificates fairly easily for Harry's parents, Mum's grandparents: Robert Reynolds, dated 7 December 1927, aged 66 years who died of heart disease, occupation railway shedman. Eliza Reynolds dated 20 July 1939, widow of Robert Reynolds, died of myocardial degeneration, arterio sclerosis and gangrene of the left leg due to arterio aclerosis. *Mum then remembered a story about her grandfather who had become very depressed and ended his life in care and that some years later her grandmother had died while having her leg amputated.*

We found a death certificate for my grandmother on my father's side of the family. Dated 25 March 1938, Elizabeth Maloney aged 76 years, wife of Charles Maloney, a general labourer. *I now knew that Granddad Maloney was still possibly alive in 1938.* Cause of death was given as myocardial degeneration and perinephritic abscess *(related to kidney)*; present at the death was her daughter S. Harrison. This meant that Dad had a sister and as he was born in 1888 we searched births surrounding this time. *This turned out to be not a bad day for finding ancestors and I was pleased because Mum was with me as she was enjoying her contribution to my research.*

We found Sarah Frances Maloney born 7 April 1894, daughter of Charles Maloney, a marine fireman, and Elizabeth Maloney, formerly Pilkington. *I have a sister called Frances.* There was also one for a William Maloney born on 14 October 1889 that proved to be Dad's brother. Grandad's occupation this time is given as steamship stoker. Another certificate we found in 1899 for a Margaret Maloney proved incorrect.

Finally on this day Mum dragged me to births surrounding 1908 even though I assured her I had searched from 1907 to 1909. We looked again in every quarter of all three years but there was nothing. Searching further found a Margery Walker. As unlikely as it may seem from the date of the certificate we tried to convince ourselves that this was Maggie.

Margery Walker was born in Ewell, a registration area of Epsom. *Mum had lived in Ewell herself as a child.* The parents listed were Albert George Walker (Nan had a brother called George), and Florence Jane Walker, formerly Oliver. Father's occupation is listed as asylum attendant. *Although I desperately wanted this to be Nan, and almost convinced myself it was, a nagging doubt stored itself in the pending tray of my brain. I also spoke with Auntie Shirley and Uncle Harry who said they knew of this certificate via some cousins of mine who had also been looking for Maggie. Although they too had doubts, they believed that it could possibly be Nan.*

I talked to other members of my family including my sister Maria who had a few years previously decided to look into Dad's family, something I was completely unaware of. Maria had looked at baptismal records at St Sylvester's in Liverpool and found several of Dad's siblings. She also found information about some of their marriages:

◆ Edward born in 1885;
◆ Charles (Dad) born in 1888;
◆ William born in 1889;
◆ Sarah born in 1894 who married and became a Harrison;
◆ John born in 1897;
◆ Elizabeth born in 1899 who married and became a Culleton; and
◆ Margaret born in 1902 who married and became a Ryan.

Edward, William and John are believed to have died young within a short space of time due to diphtheria. Indeed, we had heard on the family grapevine that there were up to five deaths at that time.

My brother Kevin and his wife Heidi decided to see if they could find the double grave of our paternal grandparents, Charles and Elizabeth Maloney, reputed to be in the same cemetery in which our sister Kathleen is buried. They acquired the grave number by phoning the cemetery concerned but could not find the grave where it was supposed to be. They visited several more cemeteries looking at similarly numbered graves before calling me in a dejected and angry state. After going over everything they had been through, which was not easy as they were both so fed up, I asked who was buried in the first grave they looked at and Heidi said, 'a couple by the surname of Harrison'. I replied, 'As in Sarah Harrison?' Kevin came back on the phone stunned that I could possibly know this. It was then that I was able to inform him, to his joint amusement and irritation, that Sarah Harrison is the daughter of Charles and Elizabeth

Moloney. The date on the grave for Sarah's husband is 1936 and as Sarah's mother had died in 1938 it must have been decided to bury Elizabeth with Sarah's husband followed by Sarah's father at some point. Sarah herself would join her husband and parents some forty years later when presumably her family had the headstone replaced.

When looking at gravestones of ancestors it is wise to think of possible descendants who may well have used the same plot and have replaced the gravestone without mention of the previous inhabitants.

I also did another search on the FamilySearch website on Mum's maternal side of the family following the Cuffley name from Mum's grandmother Eliza Cuffley and found links back to 1690. However, although these have to be checked the links look good.

My father Charles Maloney had been married previously and I had four half brothers and sisters who are all now dead, none of whom I ever met although I knew that my half brother Charles had died during the Second World War. I had heard from one of my family history magazines of a site on the Internet called the Commonwealth War Graves Commission (www.cwgc.org) and decided to have a look. I found it fairly easy to use although I had no great hopes of finding my half

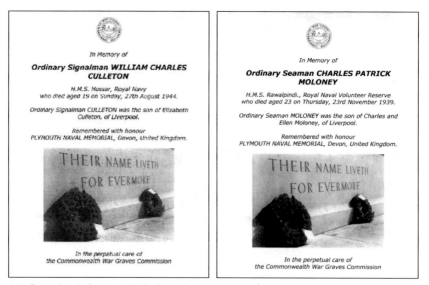

4.14   Extracts from the Commonwealth War Graves Commission web site for George Patrick Maloney and William Charles Culleton

brother. I tried under the spelling Maloney, Navy and Second World War first with no results at all so I keyed in the same information using the spelling of Moloney. Charles appeared before my eyes. Ordinary Seaman Charles Patrick Moloney, HMS *Rawalpindi*, Royal Naval Volunteer Reserve who died aged 23 on Thursday, 23 November 1939, son of Charles and Ellen (Helen) Moloney of Liverpool (see figure 4.14). It was another heart-rending moment because I can only remember hearing about Charles as a small child, and I had never really thought about him since then. But although I had never met him and there are no photographs or a grave to visit, he was my brother, and for the first time in my life I felt a personal connection between us.

My brother Michael told me that Charles fell out with Dad and volunteered into the Navy in rebellion. Sadly it was a short-lived rebellion.

> I searched the Internet for information on the *Rawalpindi*. First I keyed in The *Rawalpindi* and then Royal Navy World War 2 but there was nothing obvious. So then I keyed in 'The sinking of the *Rawalpindi*' and found a site called www.internet-promotions.co.uk (The Highland Archives). This site gave me a blow-by-blow description of the *Rawalpindi*'s sinking by a powerful warship the *Scharnhorst*. Out of 278 seamen only 38 survived. I also discovered that Edward Coverley Kennedy, the Captain of the *Rawalpindi*, was also the father of future media figure Ludovic Kennedy.

I wondered about other members of Dad's family and searched several variations looking under the names Maloney and Moloney, and then under the married names of two of Dad's sisters, Harrison and Culleton. To my utter amazement up came the name William Charles Culleton, HMS *Hussar*, Royal Navy, who died aged 19 on Sunday 27 August 1944, son of Elizabeth Culleton of Liverpool (See Figure 4.14). Apparently HMS *Hussar* was part of the British 1st Minesweeping Flotilla that were sweeping the Channel when 16 RAF rocket-firing Typhoons accompanied by a Polish squadron of Spitfires mistakenly bombed them; survivors initially were told to keep their mouths shut although ultimately there was a hearing. I cannot believe the information available – to find my half brother and cousin, Charles and William, is extraordinarily moving.

What I learned:

- A birth could be registered late, as with my mum.
- Maggie's marriage certificate with her declaration confirms that she probably did not have possession of her own birth certificate.
- The death certificate for my grandmother Elizabeth Maloney, née Pilkington, in 1938 told me that my grandfather Charles was still living at this time.
- Talking to family members about your research can bring further information as with the details of Dad's siblings I sourced from my sister.
- The grave of an ancestor can be shared and gravestones can be replaced when later family members use the same plot.
- Reading 'Family History' magazines or other material is worthwhile because you learn of other sources of information as I did with the Commonwealth War Graves website.

I now have the beginning of a family tree of my very own (see figure 4.15)!

Anger in December 2000

During this time I continued my quest for the birth certificate of my grandmother, Maggie, looking at every Walker in the final quarter of both 1907 and 1908 but she was hiding somewhere and it was beginning to irritate me badly.

4.15 Ancestors of Diane Moloney

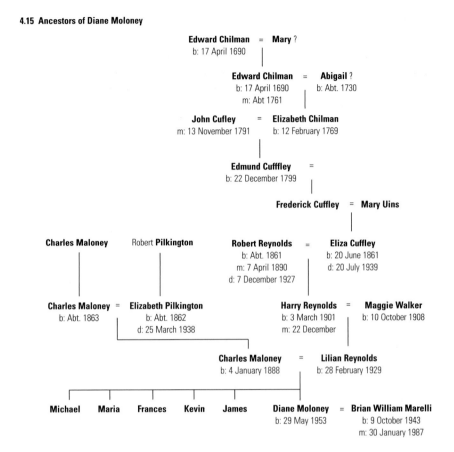

Where are you, Maggie?
(January to October 2001)

Mum said that Nan, who shall from now on be referred to as Maggie, always believed her birth date to be 10 October 1908; she was born in Epsom. Based on this information alone it was becoming apparent that I was not going to find her.

January 2001

As there appeared to be no evidence of Maggie having been born and after several discussions with my mum and aunt and uncle I decided to see if I could find the death certificate for Maggie's brother George. Apparently someone else in the family had previously carried out some research and it was believed that George married a Griffiths and both he and his wife died within a short time of each other during the 1960s.

Throughout several visits to the FRC I searched deaths and found one for a George Walker in the 1970s. I also decided to look for a birth certificate for George but could only find one possible for an Arthur George Walker born in Epsom. *Thinking about what happened with Amy Alice Plummer actually being Alice Amy Plummer I decided to order this certificate.*

I could not stop myself from looking once again for Maggie and searched through births and found myself ordering one for a Maggie Walker born in Sheffield. *I was getting desperate.*

I also checked marriages for a George Walker to a Griffiths and found one for a parish in London and one for a parish in Glamorgan. There was so little information about George. I did not even know for sure where he might have lived or if he stayed in the Epsom area so once again I had to follow up these possible leads.

The certificates arrived

The first is the death certificate for George Walker. This gentleman lived in the Epsom area, occupation market gardener; his son was present at his death. What did this mean to me? Nothing, because there were no other clues on the certificate. Phone calls to relatives asking about a possible son of George proved futile also.

The birth certificate for Arthur George Walker born in the Epsom area was a little more interesting. His father was George, occupation asylum attendant, mother Alice Walker. *My pulse picked up pace; although he was known as George his birth name could have been Arthur George.*

The birth certificate for Maggie Walker gives the parents as James and Leah Walker. *Right month and year if not the right date.* I phoned Mum willing her to tell me there had been some mention of Sheffield during her childhood, or that her grandmother was called Leah; it meant nothing to her but she did say, emphatically, that her grandmother was not called Leah. *How did she know that? Was Mum holding back on a vital piece of information?* Mum said her grandmother was called something like Azuria, Asoria or Azerora. I searched every book I could find on Christian names and the Internet trying to find a name resembling the one Mum had given me. I even read each one out to her over the phone in the hope of discovering this elusive name. Exasperatingly Mum insisted that none of the names I had found came close to what she remembered. At this point I accused her of making it up, that there was no such name and she must have dreamt it! Mum also remembered Nan saying her ancestors were French. Now I was really beginning to believe that most of what Mum had been told was fantasy. Nothing added up!

The two marriage certificates for George Walker left me cold. There was not a single piece of information that gave me any hope at all.

During this month I paid a visit to the Wirral where Mum lives and found myself at the Central Library in Liverpool looking at microfiche of births. I decided to order copies of all the Walkers born in the last quarter of 1907 and 1908. *At least I could study the births at my leisure in the hope that Maggie would spring off the page and say 'here I am'.*

Back at the FRC (a quick visit as it is my wedding anniversary and hubby is not best pleased) I decided to find and order the death certificate for Maggie. I also looked for my grandmother's birth on my father's side, Elizabeth Pilkington born about 1861, and found one registered in Prescot, close to Liverpool. My main reason for being there though was to try to find a marriage certificate for Arthur George Walker, hoping he might be married to someone called Griffiths, and found one in the 1930s.

The certificates arrived

Maggie's death certificate gave her date of birth as 9 October 1907, a different year, but I knew this to be based only on family hearsay as none of Maggie's children had any more idea of her exact date of birth than she did herself. However, with this and the other information I had collected I now believed her date of birth to be during the month of October in either 1907 or 1908, even if it wasn't registered.

The certificate for Elizabeth Pilkington is wrong. I knew this because her father was called Robert and this Elizabeth's father is called Thomas. *Scream! My research appears to be deteriorating rapidly. Was my previous success due to beginner's luck rather than ability?*

Salvation arrived in the form of the marriage certificate for Arthur George Walker of Epsom to a Martha. *This was the marriage that someone else in the family had mentioned.* One of the witnesses was Alice Taylor. *Something is wrong though.* The Arthur George whose birth certificate I had does not match the age given on this certificate. *My head began to hurt. Why was this happening?*

I spoke to Mum on the phone and read out everything on the marriage certificate for Arthur Walker. Only the name of Alice Taylor, a witness at the marriage, jogged something in Mum's memory. She remembered Maggie referring to her grandmother once as Grandmother Taylor, as she had remarried. *Poor Mum was so apologetic because she had not remembered this before but it didn't matter to me because she remembered it now; I would have kissed her had she not been 250 miles away.* A quick check of the birth certificate for Arthur George, although it wasn't the right date as per the marriage certificate, gave me the name of his mother as Alice Walker, matching the Christian name of Alice Taylor on the marriage certificate for Arthur. This meant the surname Taylor matched with Mum's information that Maggie's mother had remarried a Taylor. Perhaps Mum was mistaken about Maggie's mother's name being Azoria or whatever - maybe it was simply Alice. At least it began with the same letter.

What I had learned

- I believed I had the right marriage certificate for Maggie's brother George.
- I probably had the right birth certificate for George (Arthur) even though the year is wrong, as there were no others registered for Arthur George or George Arthur.
- I had the names of Maggie and George's parents and the Christian name began with the letter A, although not the fictitious name of Azoria, but Alice. *I was becoming happily confident I was on the right track.*

I also asked the FRC to carry out searches for Maggie and George on my behalf, for a fee, thinking that perhaps they might find something I had missed. They did not find anything either.

March 2001

I had an e-mail from Uncle Harry listing some names and addresses from an old address book he had of my grandfather's. Of the several addresses I succeeded in finding a phone number for, one was an Ann Gosling. I telephoned and explained who I was and said her address had been found in my grandfather Harry Reynolds' address book – she turned out to be my grandfather's niece. Later in the year we visited Ann and her husband Ron in Charlwood, Surrey, taking my parents with us, and although we were given lots of information about granddad's brothers and sisters Ann could not help us with Maggie. We have stayed in touch. Sadly Ann's husband Ron would pass away during the coming year. His death touched us deeply as we had only just met and been welcomed by this lovely man.

Old letters, photographs with names on, diaries, address books, Christmas cards, school reports, wedding service cards, funeral service cards and all those things parents and grandparents tend to hoard are valuable sources of information. I can remember throwing out old address books and wedding service cards and I can remember Mum having clear-outs of drawers full of what was deemed rubbish. If only we could go back in time!

With regards to your own personal photographs, write the names of your relatives on the back of family photos today. We inherited a great deal of old photographs from Bert, some were written on and some we were able to work out who was who. Sadly there are several group photos that we can only guess at because there is no information with them.

Believing I had found details of Maggie's brother and parents, even though I had nothing significant about Maggie, I searched for my maternal great grandfather Robert Reynolds and my paternal grandmother Elizabeth Pilkington, both of whom were born *circa* 1861. Of the two birth certificates I purchased for Robert Reynolds only one proved a possibility – the son of Robert Reynolds, a gentleman's groom, and Esther Reynolds, formerly Stevens. The only problem was this Robert was born in Rotherhithe. Of the two certificates I purchased for Elizabeth Pilkington for 1862 and 1863 neither had the father's name of Robert that I needed. *Common names cause great problems with research, as I was finding, and as the only way to ascertain whether you have the right person is to order the certificate, this in turn can be expensive.*

My pages for the last quarters for births for 1907 and 1908 arrived from Liverpool Central Library. I ordered another certificate for a Marjorie Walker from Kingston but this again proved incorrect as it did not match with anything else I had. *I was beginning to have great doubts about the evidence I had collected regarding Arthur George Walker although most of the family believed I was on the right track.*

I also found details of an Alice Walker's marriage, hoping it would be Alice Walker's second marriage, and ordered that certificate by phone but stated the groom's surname should be Taylor. It was not, so I did not get the certificate and was only charged £3.

What I did find though was a death certificate for Arthur George Walker that I already had birth and marriage details for. There is one interesting piece of information on this certificate and that is the name and address of his stepson. I sat on this information for a few days but then decided to try to trace a phone number for this possible relative. This was easy via Directory Enquiries. I dialled the number not knowing what to expect. The gentleman concerned was charming and very interested in what I had to say but he had never heard his stepfather talk about a sister called Maggie, her siblings or anyone else I had information about. He confirmed that his mother and stepfather died within a short time of each other *(as someone else in the family had previously discovered)* and also told me that his step-grandmother had worked at Epsom Racecourses. When I explained to the gentleman that I had some of his parents' certificates of birth, marriage and death he called me a 'cheeky bugger', and I suppose if they are not related I have to agree with him! When I spoke to my mother she then remembered that her mysteriously named grandmother had been a laundress, specialising in shirts for gentlemen. I called the charming gentleman back and asked him if his step-grandmother had ever been a laundress. He said 'definitely not!' but wished me luck in my search for Maggie.

It was the most soul-destroying moment. I had so much research that fitted together, so many clues I had followed up, but much more than that I had hope that this information, although only theory, would eventually lead me to Maggie when in truth I had absolutely nothing at all. I was inconsolable. Mum was becoming worried about my well being as I was rundown, and wanted me to stop looking for Maggie for the sake of my health. I could not stop because not only would I be letting myself down, I would be letting my mum down and no matter what she said I knew this meant so much to her. We agreed that I would take a break for a while.

When searching for that elusive ancestor if you happen across names of possible living relatives you can find telephone numbers via Directory Enquiries, also available online. Concentrate perhaps at first just on the area you believe your ancestors originated from. I have always received a reasonably positive reaction from the calls I have made or letters I have written so it is worth trying. If there are a number of possibilities then draft a letter and send a copy to all concerned with a stamped addressed envelope. You will be surprised how many people are interested in family history.

May 2001

I did take a sort of break by not travelling to London and ordering certificates etc, but I found I was becoming very good at finding sites connected with genealogy or family history on the Internet.

My favourite site is www.genforum.genealogy.com. This is a forum where you can post messages asking for help relating to your family history research and which I use off and on all the time either to post messages or to read messages posted by other families researching the same name. I have had an e-mail from a lady called Maria in America who had read one of my notes and was hoping to find a Marelli link with the family; as yet we have not established that link but we have stayed in touch. I also go to GENUKI – www.genuki.org.uk – and Cyndi's List – www.cyndislist.com, both of which are very informative, giving A–Z links to other family history sites including searchable databases. While surfing the net one evening I came across a site called FreeBMD - www.freebmd.rootsweb.com. (All of these sites and more can be found in a book called *The Genealogist's Internet* by Peter Christian. Another great book is *Family and Local History Handbook* printed by the Genealogical Services Directory – www.genealogical.co.uk.) This was a real find - a project to get all the indexes I was travelling to the FRC to view onto a free online database recording births, marriages and deaths from 1837 to 1901. I spent hours, days, weeks and months trawling this site, it was fantastic but I soon became frustrated because although the records were building by the million I personally needed more records to be online. It was only in October that I realised instead of moaning about how long this volunteer project was taking to load information I could help and volunteer myself. So I did, and started transcribing in November of the same year.

All these sites and more can be found in my new book @homewithyourancestors.com or visit www.dianemarelli.co.uk

June – September 2001

We took Mum and Gary, my stepfather, on holiday to Italy, a place we love for obvious reasons, and upon our return I decided to take a break from family history. I spent the next few weeks socialising and pursuing other interests but slowly, nagging thoughts followed by sleepless nights and irritability ensued, until my brain began computing family history facts again and it dawned on me that I was ready for action once more.

October 2001

Mum now believed I had given up on my search for Maggie but secretly I was trying to think of a new approach. If only the 1901 Census was on line or if only I could purchase the 1891 Census for Surrey on CD then I could look up the mysterious, strangely named Azuria or whatever her name was, mother of the equally mysterious Maggie. I could not get that stupid Azuria out of my head, but I wanted to, badly.

Mum had phoned a few weeks previously telling me something else from her childhood. For the record my mum was being asked to recall memories of her childhood of over seventy years ago in some instances, and had blocked many things out for personal reasons. So although I wanted this information I also knew it was difficult for my mum. Mum remembered that Maggie had once asked her brother George if she was a Taylor or a Walker – she must have been confused when she found out that her mother had remarried. Maggie was told that she was definitely a Walker. Apparently she asked how he could be so sure and was told it was best she did not know! Mum also said that Maggie would not talk about her birth mother because she had no feelings for her. Well, at least now I believed there was a mother so Maggie was not an orphan, although the information disturbed me and I was beginning to worry. What was I delving into? Yet at the same time I still wanted to know the answers. I also learned that Maggie had told Mum that she was fostered out to a farm in the Reading area during or just after the First World War. She was happy at the farm and talked about her time there fondly. Here Maggie had some schooling at home because of ill health mainly, a bad case of eczema that she had throughout her childhood. (As a child I was also covered in eczema.)

Uncle Harry's health was deteriorating so determined to find Maggie I took a day off work and went back to the FRC. I decided to order any female Walkers I could find born in Epsom around the time of Maggie's estimated birth year keeping my eye out obviously for an Amelia Walker also. My search brought the following:

◆ Florence Walker, daughter of Albert George Walker and Florence. I already had one of the children of this marriage.
◆ Evelyn Amy Walker, daughter of Albert George Walker and Florence again! Why couldn't I have a straightforward family like this?

◆ Amy Elizabeth Walker, daughter of George Walker and Annie Walker, formerly Turner. Annie Walker only meant the Rover's Return from *Coronation Street* to me but Turner meant nothing. I spoke to my mum who told me that Maggie had mentioned a family called Turner but she was not sure if they were relatives or family friends. Maybe this Annie Walker, née Turner was a connection to Maggie.

◆ The next two births were for Ada Lily Walker and Annie Lilian Walker who were both daughters of George Walker and Annie Walker again. If only one of their children could be George – the father had the right name and the mother's name began with the letter A. Maybe this is the family. If this were the right family though, surely all of their children would be registered, so why would they leave out Maggie and George unless they were very much younger or older than I had imagined – it did not make sense!

I also ordered a marriage certificate, after searching over a period of ten years from 1902 for a George Walker from Epsom hoping to find Maggie's parents. This proved unlikely as both this George and his wife were already 40 years old and there were no further clues on the certificate.

I did not find an Amelia Walker.

I felt I could not waste any more time looking for Maggie and siblings at the FRC and decided to order more copies of the index pages from the Central Library in Liverpool. I sent an e-mail and went quite mad ordering Walker births from 1909 to 1912 for all quarters and the first three-quarters of 1907 and 1908 as I already had the last quarters for these years. I also decided to investigate the Taylor issue because how could I be sure that George had given Maggie the correct information, especially as he obviously did not want Maggie to know about her background? I also ordered Taylor births from 1906 to 1909 for all quarters. This was going to be a lot of work for the Central Library because they asked me at first to try locally but there was nowhere else that I could find who would offer this service. It was only when I was eventually given the costs I decided to cut out the Taylor births and go just for the Walkers. This cost approximately £48.

While still waiting for the above pages from the Central Library to arrive I posted a note about Workhouses on the Genforum site as Mum had called again to say perhaps I should try and find out if records for such institutions were kept anywhere. At the same time I surfed the net and found a site called 'The Story of Workhouses' by Peter Higginbotham on www.workhouses.org.uk – what a wealth of information this proved to be and it also gave me links to researching workhouse records. Simultaneously I received a message from a kind person on Genforum also pointing me in this direction.

With information gleaned from the workhouse site I e-mailed Surrey History Centre in Woking where the workhouse records for Surrey were kept, on 24 October 2001. I told them everything I knew about Maggie, giving estimated dates of 1912-22, the time it was likely she was a resident in the workhouse, hospital or orphanage, based on another conversation with my mother. I explained everything I had done, everything my mum remembered and why my research was becoming a matter of urgency, asking the question if I could view the records or if I paid someone would they look for me. This was a long shot to me as I could be not certain about whether Maggie had lived in a workhouse because all she had said to Mum was that she had been in hospital a great deal and it was Mum who believed she had lived in a workhouse.

What I learned

◆ Old family address books can prove useful.
◆ Trawling the Internet constantly is a worthwhile exercise.
◆ Sometimes taking a break is a good idea.
◆ Family history is an expensive hobby but if you want results you have to be prepared to spend.
◆ It is worth using message board websites such as Genforum as there is always someone willing to help you.

Sadly on 29 October 2001 Uncle Harry passed away. It was a difficult time for all, not least Auntie Shirley and their only child Paula. Shirley told me that Harry never lost faith that I would find Maggie, his mother.

The workhouse

(November to December 2001)

November 2001

On 9 November 2001 I received a completely unanticipated e-mail from Jane Tombe of the Surrey History Centre. Below is an edited transcription:

9 November 2001
Dear Ms Marelli

Family History: Maggie Walker

Thank you for your e-mail of 24 October.

I checked the creed register (Ref BG3/42/4) for the Board of Guardians (who administered the workhouses) which list the religious creed of the inmates and found a Maggie Walker born 10 October 1907 *(so she was only a year out)* who was admitted on 30 December 1922 and discharged 24 February 1924. Her religion is given as Primitive Methodist. I checked the admission register (BG3/36/31) for 30 December 1922 and this confirmed these details and listed her as a child and her occupation as domestic servant. She was admitted to the workhouse by order of the Board of Guardians and it was remarked that she had been returned from fosterparents.

I also found a Millie Walker in the admission register (BG3/36/30) who was born 20 August 1904. She was admitted on 1 January 1921 and was also listed as Primitive Methodist. Her occupation is given as Housemaid and the record states that she was put on an invalid diet when she arrived and described as temporarily disabled.

All Board of Guardians records covering the workhouses are closed to public inspection for 100 years. However, I hope that the above information will help you in your search for Maggie Walker's birth certificate. It may also be worth your while contacting Epsom Methodist Church to see if they have any baptism registers relating to this period.

Yours sincerely
Jane B. Tombe

Stunned and over-emotional I called Mum and read out the contents of the e-mail to her. I cannot express our mixed feelings about this new information. Not only did we have evidence that Maggie spent time in the workhouse but we also had information about her elder sister.

I should note that I was extremely lucky to have been given this information from the Surrey History Centre. For the record I should make it clear that not all minutes for all workhouses exist and those that do exist are not always indexed so sometimes searches can be lengthy processes with little or no success. I was lucky that the records I was interested in did exist and were indexed and that the Surrey History Centre had time to look on my behalf. The Surrey History Centre does provide a paid service for research details of which can be found on their website: www.surreycc.gov.uk/surreyhistoryservice.

I now had another birth date for Maggie, 10 October 1907, which nearly matched the birth date on her death certificate of 9 October 1907, even though I had family information that she was born on the 10 October 1908. I also had a birth date for Millie (Amelia) of 20 August 1904. *Although it was Maggie's birth details I desperately needed to find there was some solace in that I might at least find her sister Millie.*

Frustratingly the pages I had paid for and ordered from the Central Library in Liverpool were now useless because I needed the earlier years of Walker births. In desperation I then contacted my team leader from FreeBMD asking him if he knew how or where other than from the Central Library Liverpool I could purchase the pages I required. He said he would investigate for me. *What a star!*

Following Jane Tombe's advice I contacted the Methodist Church in Epsom and although they responded quickly they were unable to find any records of Maggie, Millie (Amelia) or George.

To keep my spirits up I ordered three certificates that I had found on the FreeBMD site for the Reynolds family in the hope of a bit of success from somewhere but sadly they were incorrect. Naturally there was nothing related to the Walkers that could help me on this site as it only held records up until the end of the nineteenth century.

That Saturday I thought there was only one thing to do so I headed back to the FRC looking for Maggie and Millie (Amelia) and George. All I found was the birth certificate for a Maggie Walker of Salop. Naturally this was not my Maggie but again I had to order the certificate if only to rule it out.

The only other certificate I found that day was another marriage of a George Walker to an Annie. These were the parents of children I had already found so it was conceivable that they had other children but perhaps elsewhere in the country, as I could find no other children in Epsom. There was nothing indexed for an Amelia, Millie or similar for the birth date of August 1904.

I e-mailed Jane at the Surrey History Centre again on 14 November 2001, reporting that although I had returned to the FRC I still could find nothing relating to Maggie or her family and also that the Epsom Methodist Church had drawn a blank. I asked her if the records supplied the names of the parents who put their children into the workhouse or if she could point me in the right direction. Actually I think I pleaded with Jane and I also phoned to ask if I could go through the records myself. Sadly I could not.

Highly charged emotionally, I phoned the SoG (Society of Genealogists) and explained my plight, in detail and somewhat irrationally, to a charming gentleman who suggested that Maggie's birth had not been registered and it was a sad story he had heard often. *I was distraught. This could not be the end, and I could not give up.* He then suggested that now that I had a birth date of 10 October 1907 from the workhouse records, my only option would be to search for all the Maggies or derivatives of that name under every surname in that quarter. At least then I could decide whether it was financially viable to order all the certificates I might find during my search. However, this could prove not only futile, but also expensive. *What if Maggie was born in Reigate or Redhill or Banstead or Kingston? How could I be sure she was born in Epsom? Just because she spent time in the Epsom workhouse it did not prove she was born in Epsom.* He also explained I could view births on microfiche at the SoG and would at least be sitting down in relative calm. It was not what I wanted to hear. I wanted a miracle, an answer to my problem – it was all getting too much. I decided to think about the suggested option, but not for long.

The following Saturday I found myself sitting in the SoG doggedly looking at microfiche for the final quarter of 1907, even though Maggie could still have been born in 1908. I decided to go with the year on

Maggie's death certificate and the workhouse records that both recorded the birth year as 1907. I arrived at opening time and worked solidly for over five hours reading every index on every page, noting down every female born in the Epsom area for that quarter and by late afternoon I had only reached the end of the Cs. I felt crushed by the thought of what lay ahead. I was tired mentally before I started searching without reading the tiny lettering of microfiche for such a long time, plus I knew in my heart I had not done a thorough job for the last two hours because I was so tired. My eyes fogged with tears. I had to get out of there, it was all becoming too much. I grabbed a taxi fighting my emotions all the way to Waterloo only to embarrassingly start crying while waiting for my train. I called Brian from the train but could not speak. It was a dreadful moment for me because I was beginning to confront failure, something that I am not very good at, and I had failed Mum and Uncle Harry.

The Society of Genealogists has a comprehensive website www.sog.org.uk but for those of you without the Internet the address is: 14 Charterhouse Buildings, Goswell Road, London EC1M 7BA.

Their library holds civil registration on microfiche, Census records and over 9,000 copies of parish registers, poll books, directories and numerous other items that will be of interest to family historians.

I should also note that even if you do not have the Internet at home you can visit Internet cafés or will find Internet access at some History Centres and other public organisations such as libraries. You can freely access all the websites I have listed and more for a small charge.

On 20 November – Bert's birthday coincidentally – I received another incredible e-mail from Jane at the Surrey History Centre. The edited transcription is as follows:

20 November 2001
Dear Ms Marelli

Family History: Maggie Walker

Thank you for your e-mail of 14 November and your telephone call last week.

I checked the Board of Guardians minutes (Ref BG3/11/38) and found an entry dated August 1922 for Millie Walker which reads:

Millie Walker

Mr William George Taylor appeared before the Board and made application to be allowed to take his step-daughter, Millie Walker, who had been adopted by the Board, out of the Institution. Resolved that consent be given.

I searched the minutes for two months prior to Maggie's admission for any further clues but sadly could find nothing listed. I also checked minutes for two months either side of her discharge date (24 February 1924) but I'm afraid I drew a blank here as well.

I am sorry to disappoint you after such a good start. Hopefully you will be able to find out a bit more through your research into the Methodist connection. I wish you every success.

Yours sincerely

Jane B. Tombe
for County Archivist

My goodness, just when I was about to give up another amazing lead. Jane might have felt this information was disappointing but I certainly did not. What a wonderful thing she had done for us! I replied telling her just that.

The William Taylor above had to be the second husband of Maggie's mother. Strange that William the stepfather should turn up to take Millie from the Workhouse, not the mother, but how could he leave Maggie there? Perhaps Millie was beginning to get ill, as rumour had it she died young. Even so, why take one child and not the other?

With my head spinning I booked another day off work to visit the FRC to look for William Taylor's marriage in the Epsom area. (Luckily where I work is a family-run company who are also friends and they knew what I was going through. In fact they are now researching their family.) My thinking was that if I could find the second marriage of Maggie's mother to a William Taylor it might provide a clue to her identity and her children. The only sensible way I could think of to search for this marriage was to look under the name William Taylor, as I still had no confirmation that Maggie's mother was a Walker. I searched from 1906 to 1922 and out of the thousands of Taylor marriages ordered four more certificates.

The certificates arrived

There were four William Taylors but none of them had wives with a Christian name beginning with the letter A, although that alone is debatable, as we have still not found a name that sounds like the one my mother believes it to be, Azoria or whatever. Neither did any of the wives have the surname of Walker, Taylor or even Turner, and they were all spinsters so it was not as if any of them had been married several times which would have explained a differing surname.

What was left for me to check? Should I consider going back to the SoG to continue my search for Maggies born in the third quarter of 1907? If I did it would probably mean that I would have to order dozens of certificates and maybe find that the whole exercise was useless and I then would have to do the same thing again for 1908. Could I face another Saturday, or many Saturdays, like the last or would I cry! Maybe I should keep looking for Taylor marriages other than William, or should I look at all Taylor, Walker and Turner marriages from 1900 to 1925 for females with strange Christian names beginning with the letter A? It was a nightmare. I suppose I could look for the other children of Annie and George Walker, if indeed there were any more, in other parts of the country but that would mean looking for children born before 1907. Would that be a waste of time as there would be thousands of Walkers born during this period? There is a slim possibility that I might find George or Amelia, as I could not find Maggie, who was supposedly born prior to 1907! To hell with it all; I am going to wait for the 1901 Census to come online. At least with the Census I will be able to search in the comfort of my own home for the various Walkers, Taylors and Turners in Surrey, and the rest of the country if need be for the mysterious 'A' person!

…Waiting for the 1901 Census to come online is a bad idea because this is me I am talking about, Mrs Too Impatient. It is no good, I will have to beg the Surrey History Centre to let me view every record they had for Epsom workhouse – surely they could break the hundred-year rule just once! I know what I'll do, I'll seek legal help to find Maggie; that is my right as her descendant regardless of the hundred-year rule. I will write to all the authorities – the Prime Minister if necessary. Surely if you can prove that you are only trying to source your own family history, a basic human right, then you should be allowed to view records within the last hundred years. I bet Uncle Harry knows all the answers now – he is probably with Maggie at this moment. Perhaps I should ask for his help.

Mum was as frustrated as I was but also worried that I was going to make myself ill, although on the quiet Auntie Shirley kept me motivated by her total faith that I would find Maggie. I went through all the information I had collected whether old or new, over and over, spreading certificates before me hoping for inspiration, looking at index pages until I was pulling my hair out. There was only one thing that popped eerily into my head and that was the name of Maggie Brown, one of the few varying surnames I had collected that awful day at the SoG. I went to bed that night thinking about that name: Maggie Brown, Maggie Brown – it was driving me mad. It was stupid to even consider that this could be my Maggie as I had only carried out a search from A to C; what about D to Z? I should wait until I complete that mode of research before I make any more rash decisions. I woke the following morning thinking about Maggie Brown and arrived at work annoyed with myself and irritable. This was ridiculous. I even asked Sue, my friend, to stop me if I tried to order another certificate. She said nothing would stop me if I decided to order it and that I should trust my instinct as it had not let me down before. I ordered the certificate and miraculously the name Maggie Brown faded from my mind.

On the morning of 29 November, one month *(coincidentally or otherwise)* after Uncle Harry died, the post arrived including one brown envelope addressed to me. As I was late for work I carried the envelope back to the bedroom to collect my handbag and it was only then it occurred to me that it had to be the birth certificate for Maggie Brown! Completely nonplussed I wondered if I should open the envelope now or at the office. I ripped the envelope open, irritated because I was late, and read the name of Maggie Brown, the name of her father and the name of her mother and sat down on the bed for a brief moment. I went numb, my brain would not compute, so I put the certificate back in the envelope and went to work. A couple of hours later with the morning rush over I said quietly to Sue, 'I think I have my grandmother's birth certificate.'

The certificate

The certificate read:

Maggie Brown born on 10 October 1907, daughter of Albert Edward Brown.

How could I be sure it was my nan, Maggie? Firstly because of the date of birth and secondly because the Christian name of her mother is Asar Zora with the surname Brown, formerly Walker!

I phoned Mum and asked her if the name Asar Zora meant anything to her and she screamed down the phone to me that it was the name of her grandmother. She was so excited I had the name at last I was nearly tempted not to tell her at that moment about the birth certificate for fear she would have a heart attack. Choking back tears I did tell her though and her joy was staggering, a moment neither of us will ever forget.

When I calmed down, recovered my mental composure and chilled for a couple of days basking in the glory of my success, something dawned on me. Nearly everything Mum had told me had been proved to be correct:

◆ That Maggie was born in Epsom;
◆ That Maggie had lived in a workhouse;
◆ That Maggie had a sister called Amelia who was also in the workhouse;
◆ That Maggie's mother was called something similar to Asar Zora;
◆ That Maggie had a brother called George – yet to be proved but I now believe in his existence;
◆ That Maggie's mother remarried a Taylor;
◆ That Maggie's birth date was more or less when she said it was;
◆ That Maggie was unsure about her surname even though she thought it was Walker or Taylor – her mother was a Walker who became a Taylor, so maybe Maggie has an instinct about this;
◆ That Maggie did exist.

The only thing not proved was the bit about French ancestry, which does not look likely with surnames such as Walker and Brown. Still, you can't have it all!

What I learned

◆ Never take family information for granted.
◆ When you have a strong gut feeling about something can you really afford to ignore it?

I received an e-mail from my FreeBMD contact that had found someone to help me get the pages of births I required; I e-mailed back thanking him and informing him of my good news.

> I cannot emphasise enough what a wonderful invention the Internet has become in the world of family history. I hardly knew anything about the Internet when I first started my research; I did not even know I had a modem on my home computer! Now I wonder how I would have coped without it. I used to think you always need a website address to look something up, then one day I simply typed in Genealogy and Family History and went on from there, adding interesting sites to my favourites list and gradually working through the sites to find information of interest. Also when I find a page of information I highlight and print the selected text I'm interested in or highlight the text and copy it into my word processing package. You do not need to be an expert to work the net.

December 2001.
One journey over but another just begun

What joy it was to enter December, knowing I had just given my mum the best Christmas present in the world: Maggie Brown alias Walker, you little tinker! Now when I look at Maggie's photograph I see only a mischievous smile (see figure 6.1).

I promised Brian that in December I was going to put everything to one side and not carry out any more research until January. It was the least I could do especially when he had been so supportive. Except of course for the coming Saturday!

6.1 Maggie Brown (alias Walker) and grandchildren

A guilty aside: I felt I should try to find some more information on Brian's side of the family and attempted to find the birth certificate for the mother of Amy Plummer again, Martino's second wife. I found one certificate for a Susan Jordan and although it was in the wrong part of the country I ordered it. That certificate for Susan is incorrect as was the other one I had ordered on a whim for an unnamed male Jordan in the hope he might be a relation of Susan's.

Back on the case the first certificate I looked for was, obviously, Maggie's mother. I found it easily enough but the spelling of her Christian name is Asor Zoar. I also searched for George and Amelia, Maggie's siblings. I found Amelia under the surname Brown but could not find George. *I am beginning to think that George was not a brother of Maggie's but another relative, as there was no mention of him having been at the workhouse.*

I decided to try to find a marriage certificate for Asor Zoar under her surname of Walker but failed miserably, so I tried under the name of Albert Edward Brown and found one only for 1907.

The certificates arrived

The marriage certificate for Albert Edward Brown turned out to be incorrect.

Next was the birth certificate for Amelia Brown dated 20 August 1904, as per the information from Surrey History Centre. Parents Albert Brown and Add Zord *(what?)* formerly Walker. The father Albert registered the birth, which probably explains the spelling of Asor Zoar.

The best certificate was for Asor Zoar, as she will now be rightfully known, dated 27 February 1883. Daughter of Charles George Walker, a stationary engine driver, and Mary Ann Walker, formerly Pudvine. Pudvine! What sort of name is that? Of great interest was the address of Milk House Gate, Guildford. Brian and I used to live in Guildford.

I was straight on the phone to Mum who laughed excitedly at the name Pudvine and could not believe that I had been shopping, for several years nearly every Saturday in Guildford, walking in the footsteps of my ancestors without knowing. I had history, Mum had history, and my whole family had history – what a wonder history is, especially when it is your own.

Extract from the 1881 Census

Dwelling:	Postford Farm Barn			
	Census Place:	Albury, Surrey, England		
	Source:	FHL Film 1341182 PRO Ref RG11 Piece 0775 Folio 19 Page 2		
	Marr	Age	Sex	Birthplace
Frederick PUDVINE M		44	M	Wonersh, Surrey, England
	Rel:	Head		
	Occ:	Farm Labourer		
Maria PUDVINE M		33	F	Shalford, Surrey, England
	Rel:	Wife		
	Occ:	Laundress		
Emma PUDVINE U		16	F	Worplesdon, Surrey, England
	Rel:	Daur		
	Occ:	General Servant Out Of Place		
George PUDVINE		14	M	Guildford, Surrey, England
	Rel:	Son		
	Occ:	Farm Labourer		
Eliza PUDVINE		12	F	Guildford, Surrey, England
	Rel:	Daur		
Ellen PUDVINE		4	F	Hambledon, Surrey, England
	Rel:	Daur		

6.2 Extract from the 1881 Census

I searched the 1881 Census and put in the name Pudvine and found only one family of that name – which was not really surprising but what a relief to be researching an unusual name again (see figure 6.2). Surely the Frederick Pudvine and family detailed were relations?

I had an e-mail from my sister Maria early in December who had carried out some research on the name Asor Zoar. It read:

> I found Asor and Zoar both from the Bible as we thought. Zoar is a town that was destroyed by God, like Sodom and Gomorrah – Lot was told to leave there by God. Lot went into a cave with his two daughters who seduced him and started off the tribe of Moab (Genesis). Strangely enough on the same page I came across Asor talking about research in Moab country, supposed to be near Canaan and where Moses died. Searching further I found Asor in the Bible in Hebrew text. The Asor was believed to be a ten-stringed musical instrument in the Book of Psalms.

Well, I wonder how Asor's parents came to choose such a name for their daughter?

I resisted the temptation to spend the whole of December at the FRC but searched the FreeBMD site and found two other Pudvines, Mary born in 1860 and Ada born in 1883. I also found a possible birth certificate for a Charles George Walker. Playing around with the spelling of the surname I found Henry Pudwine *(Pudwine, even more hysterical)* possibly married to an Emily Voller in 1858 in Guildford, and an Alfred Frederick Pudwine born in 1862 in Guildford.

I searched the FamilySearch site and found a Charlotte Pudvine of Worplesdon *(where I also used to live)*, christened in 1867, daughter of Frederick Pudvine and Harriet and also another record for Edwin Pudvine of Worplesdon, christened in 1867, son of Frederick and Harriett *(sic)*. I also had a look for Susan Jordan, Brian's two times great grandmother and mother of Amy Plummer. I found her: Susanna Jordan born on 13 September 1835 at Melksham, parents Richard – correct father's name – and Harriot Jordan. *This find thrilled me most but it meant that Susan is not 41 as per the 1881 Census but actually 46, about ten years older than her husband William Plummer, which is why I could find no record of her birth at the FRC.*

Remembering the National Burial Index CD that I had purchased I searched under the names Pudvine and Pudwine and found the following:

◆ Charles Pudwine, aged 22, burial date 1848, recorded in St Mary, Guildford;
◆ Stephanie Pudwine, aged 6 days, burial date 25 September 1835, recorded in St Peter and St Paul, Albury, Surrey;
◆ William Pudwine, aged 19, burial date 1848, recorded in St Mary, Guildford;
◆ William Pudwine, aged 53, burial date 1849, recorded in St Mary, Guildford.

These four Pudwines must be from the same family and how sad that all of them died within such a short time of each other.

Sue at work also discovered a living Pudvine – perhaps I would contact this person at some point.

I decided to order only the two Pudvine certificates for now, and the one for Charles Walker.

The certificates arrived

The first birth was for Mary Pudvine dated 1 July 1860, daughter of Frederick Pudvine, an agricultural labourer, and Harriett (sic) Pudvine, née Voller. *The birth certificate for Asor Zoar has the mother recorded as Mary Ann – but because of the surname Pudvine I'm fairly confident that I now have Maggie's grandmother on her mother's side.*

The next birth was for Ada Pudvine dated 25 May 1883, daughter of Frederick Pudvine and Maria Pudvine, formerly Webber. *It seems likely that Frederick married twice as this child was born to the Frederick and Maria I found on the 1881 Census as opposed to Frederick and Harriet who are the parents of Mary above.*

The last birth was for Charles George Walker dated 26 September 1860, son of Charles Walker, a railway labourer, and Ellen Walker, formerly Lee. *This had to be Maggie's grandfather but a marriage certificate was needed to check dates etc. It just dawned on me he would be on the 1881 Census – I am so slow at times.*

The 1881 Census revealed the following information:

Dwelling: Milkhouse Gate, Guildford Holy Trinity, Surrey.

Ellen Walker, Head, a widow, aged 40, born in Petworth, Sussex.

Charles Walker, Son, unmarried, aged 20, occupation General Labourer, born in Guildford, Surrey.

John Walker, Son, aged 12, born in Shalford, Surrey.

Rose Walker, daughter, aged 8, born in Guildford, Surrey.

Florence Walker, daughter, aged 5, born in Guildford, Surrey.

This added information told me that Maggie's great grandfather, Charles Walker, had died some time between the conception of his last child, Florence, and the 1881 Census taken in April of the same year.

6.3 Ancestors of Diane Moloney

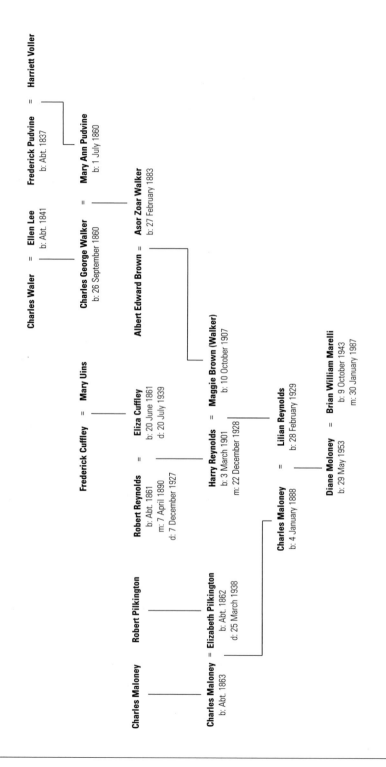

Finally for December I looked up another Internet site I had found called The Newspaper Detectives - www.newspaperdetectives.co.uk. *(I store every interesting site in my favourites)*. (When looking for information on the Internet just type in what it is you are looking for, i.e. newspaper archives as I did in this instance.) This site had an index of news stories from 1864, 1865 and 1866 from the Surrey Advertiser, although it now includes the year 1867. Up until this time the site was of no real help to me although it was interesting, which is why I copied it to my favourites. To my utter disbelief there was an index for Emily Pudwine dated 21 April 1866 and for another Pudwine dated 10 November 1866. They read as follows:

◆ 21 April 1866, Emily Pudwine, Guildford, a wife, and a policeman, assault, fined 20s;

◆ 10 November 1866, Pudwine, Guildford, drunk, 14 day prison.

This had to be the Emily who was married to Henry that I had found marriage details for on the FreeBMD site. I had read somewhere that in family history it is a sad family that has not at sometime had their name in the newspapers. Well, although what I found could not be classed as something to be proud of, I did not care. It both thrilled and amused me and suddenly brought two possible ancestors to life. *I must try to find out how I can get copies of the full stories.*

Brian and I spent Christmas with Mum and Gary, taking with us copies of the certificates and a family tree, something Mum thought she would never have – it was magic (see Figure 6.3).

What I learned

◆ If I had failed to find Maggie then I would have been unable to research any of my family history on her side of the family beyond her marriage.
◆ Never again would I think of my family as unexciting.
◆ There are amazing coincidences when researching your family such as finding I had moved 250 miles from Liverpool, or the Wirral where my family now lives, to a place where once upon a time my ancestors had lived.

- Sometimes you have to search a source several times before you find something, i.e. the Census or, in the case of Susan Jordan, the FamilySearch site.
- Some purchases of Census or christening records on CD-Rom will not prove beneficial until further along in your research.
- Without trawling the Internet I would never have found the Newspaper Detectives website and up until now I had never thought of newspapers as a source.

Meet the Pudwines
(January to April 2002)

January and February 2002

I had been ticking off the months, then days and then hours to when the 1901 Census was about to come online and I could not sleep the night before because I was so excited. Well, what an anticlimax! We all know what happened there! I was bitterly disappointed and a lot more but my reaction over this particular 'non-great' event is best left undocumented as likely to cause offence.

On 3 January I was astounded to find another e-mail from Surrey History Centre. The edited transcription goes as follows:

3 January 2002
Dear Ms Marelli

Family History: George Walker

Thank you for your e-mail of 2 December.

We had a very quiet week on the run up to Christmas and so I was able to co-opt a colleague to trawl through all the minutes and Creed Registers of the Board of Guardians for Epsom between the years 1907 and 1920 looking for George Walker. In doing so, we not only found him but also more information relating to Maggie and Millie.

The first reference we found was from an earlier Creed Register (Ref BG3/42/1) and an entry dated 1 August 1908. It refers to the first admission of Maggie Walker and lists her mother as Nora Walker of 223 Hook Road, Epsom. Later that year, on 23 November, Edith Walker and George Walker were admitted. I checked the admission registers for these dates (BG36/36/26) and found that Maggie was listed as 'sick' when she was admitted. George was listed as being born in 1904 and Edith in 1902. Interestingly enough, their religion at this time was listed as Church of England.

In the minutes of 10 May 1911 (Ref BG3/11/29) there is a note which reads:

Re Children Walker

We recommend that steps be taken for the adoption of Maggie and Millie Walker, the children of Nora Walker under the Poor Law Act 1899. (Report was resolved and adopted.)

A further note in the minutes of 21 May 1913 (Ref. BG3/11/31) reads:

Re Millie Walker

Read letter dated 19th inst. From the Invalid Children's Aid Association stating that this child was well and quite fit to go to school. Resolved that the suggestion of the Home be agreed to.

Later that year there is a report in the Minutes of 3 December 1913 (also Ref. BG3/11/31) which states:

Re Walker Children

Read Medical report from the Invalid Children's Aid Association with regard to these children which was considered very satisfactory.

We could find nothing listed for the Walker children until 30 April 1919 where further minutes (BG3/11/35) state:

Re Maggie Walker

Read letter from Mrs Goodchild asking the guardians to increase the amount given to her in respect of the boarding out of this girl. In consequence of the increased cost of medical necessaries and also enquiring whether the board would have an objection to her taking charge of two girls from the Dr Barnado's Homes.

Resolved that the sum paid to Mrs Goodchild be increased from 8/- to 10/6 weekly, and that provided that the Invalid Children's Aid Association raise no objection to her taking two girls from Dr Barnado's Homes the board offer no objection.

Then two years later the minutes of 9 November 1921 (BG3/11/37) read:

Maggie Walker

Read letter dated 7th instant from the Wantage Union stating that this girl had been compelled to leave her situation on account of eczema and asking the guardians to authorise the payment of the usual Boarding Out Allowance to her. Resolved that authority be given for the payment of 10/6 weekly and 30/- per quarter for clothing.

Since the earlier Creed Register had listed their religion as Church of England I checked the three parish churches for Epsom: St Martin's, St Barnabas and Christ Church, for any evidence of the Walker family. If Nora Walker did have any of the children christened, it does not seem to have been in Epsom.

I really do think that we have exhausted all the avenues we can. It would seem that the Walker children spent time in and out of the workhouse and boarded out to foster parents. I hope this gives you more fuel for your search through the GRO indexes. I wish you lots of luck and a very Happy New Year.

Yours sincerely

Jane B. Tombe

It was all too emotive. Maggie was only ten weeks old when first placed in the workhouse and it seems as though she probably spent most of her childhood there. It was difficult explaining this latest information to my mum, but although she was devastated by the thought of her mother having such a dreadful childhood it also helped her to understand so much more about Maggie.

I looked again at Peter Higginbotham's Internet site on the workhouse and the more I read the more I hurt for Maggie but the more I understood her and the life she must have had in the workhouse, never mind 'The Great Depression' and the Second World War. Maggie never mentioned the workhouse to Mum, but said she was in hospital a lot – denial perhaps or maybe embarrassment. I was able to help Mum understand her too and she at last was able to come to terms with her own childhood. For the first time in her life Mum knew about her mother's childhood, information she was never privy to while Maggie lived.

An aside: Another thing Mum was right about was that Maggie did live part of her childhood in the Reading area. Was it Mrs Goodchild that had a farm? This was the only time during Maggie's childhood that we know she was happy. I must see if I can track Mrs Goodchild down at some point.

I personally have mixed feelings about the workhouse. I hate the fact that my grandmother, Maggie, through no fault of her own was forced to live in a workhouse, never knowing the comfort of a normal family upbringing. But if it hadn't been for the workhouse would she have survived? I suppose it is easy to judge parents who could do such a thing to their children, having been brought up in a close and loving family myself, but I was not there. I do not know the circumstances that drove Asor Zoar to take her children to the workhouse – maybe her husband died, as she did marry again. Maybe they fell on hard times and her husband could not find work. Maybe one day I will find out but until then I prefer to believe Asor Zoar had no choice. I still have not found the marriage certificate of Asor Zoar to Albert Brown.

I was sure I read in one of the family history magazines or something similar about being able to access archived British newspapers online. This is similar, I suppose, to the Newspaper Detectives who are indexing, but not associated with, the local Surrey Advertiser.

It did not take long to find the site called British Online Newspaper Archives via www.uk.olivesoftware.com. By typing the keyword Workhouse into the search facility located on the home page I found hundreds of articles among which were two very interesting ones that gave both sides of the story of life in the workhouse around the time Maggie herself had been resident in one of these establishments. I have reproduced the articles below.

The first is taken from the *Daily News* dated 16 December 1918.

THE POOR LAW GIRL

To the Editor of the *Daily News*.

Sir, – You have given space in your columns for a discussion on the Poor Law – whether or not it shall live. I have read some outside opinions and the Guardians' defence. May I give a few whispers from within, as I was brought up in a Poor Law Home?

Poor Law children are terribly mixed in rank, character, and appearance. Some have gentle feelings and kind dispositions; others show bad breeding. Some are backward scholars and others have great talents. 'The workhouse nursery is the least objectionable to visit,' so I am told by one who knows. The children look upon Guardians as men to be revered and referred to in a whisper. If one is seen coming towards the dayroom the girls are told to smile – not an easy thing to do to order – and if they are unable to do so they get into serious trouble afterwards. Has the Guardian any idea of how the children live, of the low atmosphere they breathe, or of the degrading punishments given them for very small misdeeds and mistakes?

What becomes of us? When we are fifteen we are sent into the world, of which we are ignorant, to become general servants, as if we were responsible working girls who should know what is required of us. We are not; we feel helpless and alone, besides being strangers to life's simplest ways and habits. We have never entered a shop or handled money; at every turn we find ourselves lost, in the street, kitchen, dining-room, drawing-room or bedroom; everywhere things are new and strange, and we lack the speech, manners, knowledge and courage which are so badly needed to cope with life. Our minds are, as it were, chained up through rule and discipline; individuality is unknown to us, our capabilities have no standard, and we had no sense of self or of our importance as human beings.

In consequence of this, 'Home' Girls are backward, shy, thoughtless and slow. Many of them have no taste for housework, yet all are catalogued for domestic service. These are England's special girls. What do you readers think of the Poor Law system now?

GRACE BUMPSTEED

The response came on 19 December 1918:

THE POOR LAW GIRL

To the Editor of the *Daily News*.

Sir, – Your correspondent is, no doubt, relating her own particular experience; but what would she have been if the Poor Law had not stepped in and helped her?

Experience teaches us that no child is sent to the workhouse unless the conditions of life are such that she is unable to obtain sufficient nourishment and care in the home from which she comes.

A child is taken into the workhouse, cared for, washed, clothed, and fed from infancy until it is about five years old. Then it is transferred to a cottage home, where it is located with another 30 to 25 children, and sent to the county school. The cottage homes are in the country (most of the children come from the slums). The children are not dressed in uniform; they sit side by side with other children, and have an equal chance of obtaining scholarships.

When they are about 14 two of the girls are appointed to assist the foster mother in cleaning the home, and are taught to bake, sew, knit, and darn. For further domestic training two of the eldest girls take duty in the superintendent's house, and help in all kinds of work, including waiting at the table.

When one thinks of all that is being done for these children, one cannot but wonder what would have become of them if they had not received the care and attention of the Poor Law.

A GUARDIAN

The last article talks of only the two eldest girls being trained. I wonder what training for life the others had?

I went to the FRC in search of birth details for George Brown and Edith Brown, but was unsuccessful. I also searched for the marriage of Asor Zoar to Albert Brown and was again unsuccessful. I came home with nothing. *I broke my own unwritten rule to always take some positive information away with me so that I never come home empty-handed – I was really losing it.*

At this time I decided to slow down a little and concentrate on boring stuff like reorganising the family research I had collected. I was holding everything in two main files but this was not working for me. So I split all the documents into family names and then into date order until a female got married when she would become a member of the particular family she married into, for example:

◆ Amy Plummer's birth certificate would be in the Plummer family file in date order with the other Plummers.

◆ At marriage Amy Marelli, formerly Plummer, would then become part of the Marelli file in date order with the Marelli family.

Each certificate is stored in a plastic wallet and each family is stored in a separate document file until the family grows too large and I then transfer them to ring binders. It made things so much easier for me to work this way, but each to their own.

I also spent a great deal of time searching the 1881 Census for Henry Pudvine and others but could not find Henry or anyone else that I was still looking for. I did find a family by the name of Maloney in Liverpool that could be related to my dad who was born in 1888. I also found a Mary Anne Walker working in Guildford High Street, born in 1860 in Worplesdon. I thought this could be Maggie's grandmother, Mary Pudvine, but I will need to source the marriage certificate, as I do not know at this time if Mary Anne had already married Charles Walker. If she had not maybe for some reason she was using the name of Walker as I cannot find her on the 1881 Census under the name Pudvine, Pudwine, Mary, Mary Ann, Mary Anne or Maryann.

I posted some messages on the Genforum site asking if anyone had heard of the name Pudvine or Pudwine or knew of their origins. I only had one reply telling me again about the Pudvine that my friend Sue has sourced. *I must contact them at some point.*

What I learned

◆ Family history, although amazing, can bring heart-rending results.
◆ By taking your research further and finding out more about the lives of
your ancestors via the Census, workhouse, newspapers, etc. your
ancestors will spring to life.

March 2002

I was back at the good old FRC again. I searched from 1895 to 1920 for
a marriage certificate for Asor Zoar Walker to Albert Edward Brown
under both names but could find nothing listed. *Here I go again!*

I selected some years using one of my search forms but only for the
surnames Pudvine and Pudwine, crossing through each box carefully
twice as I went for each spelling. Eventually I found a record for Henry
Pudwine in 1858 and one for Frederick Pudwine in 1859. (Frederick's
surname is spelt differently to the 1881 Census where he is a Pudvine.)

With these exciting finds my confidence returned so I looked for the
marriage of Charles Walker to Ellen, Asor Zoar's grandparents. I found it
in 1860.

Marriages were surprisingly quiet so I took the opportunity to search for
the other marriage of Asor Zoar to a Taylor, *(still a little miffed that I
could not find her marriage to Albert Brown)*. As Maggie was born a
Brown I decided to start my search from the year 1907 thinking perhaps
Albert had died and that is why Maggie ended up in the workhouse at
ten weeks of age and that Asor Zoar would have married after this date.
I found nothing under Asor Zoar's name but several possibilities under
the Taylor name and two in the right district in 1910 and 1911, one for
William and one for George William, but I could not find a
corresponding record for Asor Zoar so I ordered both certificates.

I then went to deaths because I knew there was no mention of Maggie's
grandfather Charles Walker in the 1881 Census. I assumed he had died
between 1875 and 1881 because his last child was only five years old in
1881. I found him in 1875.

I also had three death dates for Pudwines from the National Burial Index so I looked for those. I found one for William Pudwine in 1848, one for Charles Pudwine in 1848 and one for another William Pudwine in 1849. *Was this a good day or a bad one?*

I moved back to births looking for another sibling of Maggie's under the name of Edith Brown but had no luck when something occurred to me. Could Edith have been born prior to her relationship with Albert Brown and be registered under Walker? I found an Edith Walker in 1902. I looked for George Walker but could not find him.

I also selected another certificate for Mum's grandfather Robert Reynolds, this time born in Poplar, London in 1862. I wasn't sure though.

Lastly I did a blanket search under the name Voller in the hope of finding Emily who married Henry Pudwine and was involved in the incident in Guildford as per the Newspaper Detectives website. I found one for a Louisa Voller in 1858.

While waiting for the certificates I did a thorough search on the FamilySearch site, this time in the names of Pudvine and Pudwine and below is what I found:

- Susanna Pudwine, christened in Albury on 8 April 1828, parents Thomas and Harriet Pudwine;
- William Pudwine, christened in Albury on 21 July 1829, parents William and Harriet Pudwine;
- Maryanne Pudwine, christened in Albury on 11 March 1832, parents Thomas and Harriet Pudwine;
- Frederick Pudwine, christened in Albury on 27 January 1833, parents Thomas and Harriet Pudwine;
- Henry Pudwine, christened in Albury on 16 March 1834, parents Thomas and Harriet Pudwine;
- Stephen Pudwine, christened in Albury on 14 September 1835, parents Thomas and Harriet Pudwine;
- Stephen Pudwine, buried in Albury on 25 September 1835, parents Thomas and Harriet Pudwine;
- Edwin Pudvine, christened in Worplesdon on 17 September 1865, parents Frederick and Harriett (sic) Pudvine;
- Charlotte Pudvine, christened in Worplesdon on 19 July 1867, parents Frederick and Harriet Pudvine;

- Susanna Pudvine, married to Richard Bonsey on 16 November 1851, Saint Mary Guildford;
- Ann Pudwine, married to John Stevert on 15 April 1739, Saint Dunstan, Stepney, London;
- Catherine Pudvine, married to John Greenfield on 8 July 1817, Glasgow, Lanark.

The last two names are possibly related but I'm not sure and will have to check further. I had also found a Stephanie Pudwine on the National Burial Index but now think that Stephanie is a misprint and should read Stephen.

It looks like either there are two Pudwine families both married to someone called Harriet, perhaps brothers, or there is a misprint and all should read Thomas and Harriet or William and Harriet. I must check further.

Both Frederick and Henry have the same parents regardless of whether one is Thomas or William, so they must be brothers and quite likely my Henry and Frederick. I must find the three death certificates for the two Williams and Charles.

The certificates arrived and it gets better all the time

The marriage was for Henry Pudwine, aged 24, dated 16 October 1858 (amended from aged 20), occupation dock labourer, to Emily Voller, aged 19 with no occupation. Henry does not state who his father is, frustratingly, but Emily's father is John Voller, an agricultural labourer. Witnesses at the wedding are Henry Rose and Mary Wye; neither Henry Rose nor Henry Pudwine could sign their names. *They were married in Guildford Register Office. How utterly amazing – this is where, 132 years later, I would marry Brian not knowing of course that my ancestors had lived in the surrounding area.* (It is quite common to find the name of a father missing off a marriage certificate if the parent is deceased, as Henry's father William was at the time of this marriage.)

The next marriage is for Frederick Pudwine, aged 23 years, dated 13 August 1859 *(if this was Henry's brother he should be 26 years)*, occupation agricultural labourer, to Harriett (sic) Voller aged 22 years. The father of Frederick is William Pudwine, deceased, occupation wheelwright. *On FamilySearch it states that Frederick's father was called Thomas!* Harriett's father is also called John Voller, as is Emily's, occupation agricultural labourer. The witnesses for the marriage were Charles Voller and Jane Voller; only Jane Voller could sign her name. They too were married at Guildford Register Office. *The more I find out the more complicated this is becoming. Did I say Brian's family was difficult, because if I did I was making it up!*

The next was for Charles Walker, aged 25 years, dated 9 January 1860, occupation labourer, to Ellen Lee, aged 20 years, with no occupation. Charles named his father as John Walker, a labourer, and Ellen named her father as John Lee, a millwright. *Thank goodness for that, some decent occupations are beginning to surface.* They were married at the Parish Church in Stoke next to Guildford. Witnesses were John Smith and Ann Hall; all were able to sign their names except for Ann Hall.

One of the Taylor marriages is incorrect but the other is startling. It is for Asar Zora (*sic*) (corrected from Asarzora) dated 1911 – it seems as though this is how she thought she should spell her name even though it is Asor Zoar on her birth certificate – aged 33 years, a spinster of no occupation. What did this mean? Was she lying or did she never marry Albert Edward Brown? It seems to me that as I can find no evidence of a first marriage the latter is the correct assumption! Again, I find myself shocked. Did people live together openly in those days? Obviously yes! Again how myopic a view I have of those times. Asar Zora married George William Taylor, not William Taylor as given on the workhouse record I had received previously. No wonder I could not find it when I tried before – more transposed Christian names or perhaps he too was christened George but chose to go by a middle name. He was aged 50 years and his occupation was bricklayer. They were both living at the same address. *A bit of a girl then our Asar Zora, or maybe she was just a victim of circumstance.* Asar Zora's father was Charles George Walker, occupation electrical engineer. George William's father was George Taylor, deceased, occupation builder. Witnesses were R. Edward Wallace and Wilfred J. Pickering; they were married at Epsom Register Office and all could write their names. My first reaction to finding this marriage is, what happened in her relationship with Albert Brown? My second reaction was why did she not claim her children back when she married George?

I decided to find the Pudwine death certificates that I had previously found information about on the National Burial Index, though I could not look for Stephen/Stephanie as s/he was born prior to 1837.

The first death certificate is for William Pudwine, aged 18 years, dated 21 May 1848, occupation labourer; Susan Pudwine was present at his death and signed with her mark. The cause of death is given as typhus for 14 days and the address as St Mary's Guildford. *Susan must have been William's sister judging by the information I have from FamilySearch yet William's father from that source is William and Susan's (Susanna) is Thomas. I'm beginning to think now that it's the same father but a misprint in records.*

The second death certificate is for a Charles Pudwine, aged 22 years, dated 6 June 1848, occupation labourer and cause of death fever for five days. The informant of death is J. R. Ames, Master of Guildford Workhouse. *The workhouse rears its ugly head again although the poor did go to the workhouse infirmary if ill.* I couldn't find any details of his birth on the FamilySearch site but this certificate gave me proof of his existence.

Sadly the next death is for William Pudwine, aged 53 years, dated 23 December 1849, occupation labourer and cause of death fever. The informant of the death is J. R. Ames, Master of Guildford Workhouse. If William and Charles are the sons of William how sad that they both died followed by their father. William is my five times great grandfather on my mother's side – how wonderful to know who he is.

The final death is for Charles Walker, aged 39 years, dated 3 April 1875, occupation labourer in Brewhouse (*sic*). The cause of death was bronchopneumonia (*sic*) for five days and present at the death was Mary Triggs, Milk House Gate. This was definitely Maggie's great grandfather as per the address for Ellen Walker, his wife, on the 1881 Census for Milk House Gate and their marriage certificate. Perhaps Mary was his married sister or a kindly neighbour looking after him while Ellen was at work?

The birth certificate I received for a Robert Reynolds was dated 23 November 1861. Although registered in 1861, he could be my mum's grandfather on her father's side but I have no other evidence as yet. It states his parents were Broughton Reynolds, occupation dock labourer, and Jane Arabella Reynolds, formerly Wilson. They were living in Bow but in the registration district of Poplar, Middlesex.

The second birth certificate is quite surprising. It is for Louisa Voller, dated 2 March 1858, daughter of Harriet Voller. The father's name is not given. Louisa was born in Guildford workhouse. If this was the Harriet Voller who married Frederick Pudvine then this child was born prior to their marriage in August 1859. Was she Frederick's child? I suppose I will never know but like to think it is a possibility.

The birth certificate I found for Edith Walker proved to be correct. Edith Annie Walker was born on 22 April 1902, daughter of Asar Zora Walker of no occupation. Not so shockingly – in fact becoming quite normal – there is no father's name given. Asor Zoar was living in Knaphill, Woking at the time. I wonder if she was sent to relatives because she was pregnant? I wish the 1901 Census would come online!

I carried out another search on the Internet and all my CDs of family history looking for other spellings of Pudwine hoping to find a Thomas, but could not find one. However, playing around with the spelling of the name Pudwine found me this: Alfred F. Pudwino? (sic), buried in 1862, St Mary, Worplesdon, aged five weeks.

My search on the Internet in FamilySearch brought me these:

◆ Emley (sic) Voller, christened 29 November 1840, in Worth, Sussex, parents John Voller and Charlotte;
◆ Harriet Voller, christened 30 September 1838, in Saint Nicholas, Guildford, parents John Voller and Charlotte.

Although born in different counties they must be sisters so I now believe that Frederick, who married Harriet, and Henry, who married Emily, wed sisters.

What I learned

◆ When unable to source a birth certificate for an ancestor, always consider looking under the maiden name of the mother.
◆ There are misprints and errors on most sources of information.
◆ Some sources will not be immediately useful in your research but may prove beneficial at a later date.

◆ When I compare how relatively straightforward researching Brian's family was to researching my own I realise now that sometimes you may be lucky and may not encounter any of the problems I have had.
◆ Those of us with working-class or poor ancestors are lucky they survived during the nineteenth century when family deaths seemed to have been as common as a cold.

I now have quite a family tree building (see figure 7.1).

7.1 Ancestors of Maggie Brown, alias Walker

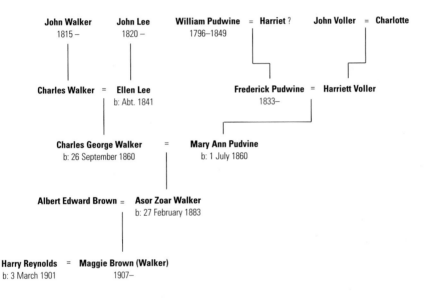

April 2002

I spoke to Mum and we talked generally about many things but somehow it prompted Mum into remembering more about her childhood, convincing me further that I should never stop Mum talking about the past or stop asking her questions.

Mum told me about her little sister called Dorothy who sadly died when Mum was about six or seven years old. Mum remembers an older woman arriving at the house dressed in a black three-quarter-length jacket and ankle length skirt with little black boots buttoned up the side.

She was also carrying a basket with a white cloth over it. Mum thought it was food of some sort, perhaps for the wake. This woman, who was very stern in appearance, came to pay her respects, Mum presumes, but said only a couple of words and left after a few minutes. When Mum asked Maggie who she was Maggie replied sharply, 'that was your Gran'. *This had to be Asor Zora because Mum had met her dad's mother, Eliza Reynolds, formerly Cuffley, previously.* Mum also remembered Maggie telling her that Asor Zora had seen Mum once before when she was a baby of about six months old. Maggie was pushing her in a pram and bumped into Asor Zora who asked Maggie what my mum was called. When Maggie said her name was Lilian, Asor Zora apparently said, 'well she doesn't look like a Lily to me'. Maggie, obviously affected by what Asor Zora had said, called Mum by the name of Peggy from that day, a name that would stick with her for life.

Mum also has fond memories of Eliza Reynolds, not that she saw her often, but she did stay with her on a couple of occasions. All she remembers is Eliza had a large gramophone with a large brass horn and a beautiful doll that she kept on top of a cabinet. Sometimes, if Mum was good, Eliza would let her hold the doll momentarily but was quick to retrieve it from her and place it safely back on top of the cabinet.

I now know something personal about two great grandmothers who I never met for obvious reasons, and it feels good to be able to add this small but real piece of information to the family history. I am certain that future generations will appreciate these little snippets of reality as much as I do.

This extra information motivated me back into action. What a month – I took days off to search plus weekends, and I'm also currently only working four days per week. There's so much to tell I really don't know where to start.

From my many trips to the FRC during this month I obtained the birth and death certificates for Mum's sister Dorothy:

◆ Dorothy May Reynolds was born on 21 August 1934, daughter of Harry William Reynolds, occupation general labourer, and Maggie Reynolds, formerly Walker, of Epsom;

◆ Dorothy May Reynolds died on 23 January 1937 aged two years, of myocardial failure by bronchopneumonia. The informant was M Reynolds, mother, of Ashtead.

During my visits to the FRC I decided to do blanket searches for Pudwine/Pudvine deaths and marriages and also the marriage of Charles Walker to Mary Ann Pudvine who are Maggie's maternal grandparents.

Marriages

Susanna Pudvine, aged 24, occupation servant, married Richard Bonsey, aged 30, occupation labourer, on 16 November 1851. Richard's father was William Bonsey, occupation labourer, and Susanna's father was William (not Thomas) Pudvine, occupation wheelwright. They were married by Banns in St Mary's, Guildford. The witnesses were Robert Wheatley and Ellen Covey; only the witnesses could sign their names.

Ann Pudwine, aged 19 years, of no occupation, married Henry Rose, aged 22 years, occupation labourer at gas works, on 14 May 1859. Ann's father was William Pudwine deceased (again not Thomas), occupation wheelwright, and Henry's father was James Rose, occupation agricultural labourer. They were married at Guildford Register Office. The witnesses were William Smith and Esther Moore. Only William and Ann could sign their names.

Lewis Pudvine — a surprise find I was not sure about but it was a 'had to have' — of full age, occupation servant, married Grace Fergusson of full age, no occupation, on 1 May 1879. Lewis gave his address as Belgrave Square, London and Grace gave hers as Park Lane, London. The father of Lewis was William Pudvine, occupation wheelwright, an amazing find, and the father of Grace was John Fergusson, occupation carrier. They were married at the Parish Church in St George's, Hanover Square. The witnesses were Christine Fergusson and John Arlidge, and all could sign their names. Wow! I was thrilled with this information, as there had been no mention of Lewis previously!

Henry Pudwine, aged 36 years, a widower, occupation labourer, married Alice Bristow, a widow, aged 43 years, of no occupation, on 9 August 1881; both were living in Castle Street, Guildford. This time Henry does give his father's name as William Pudwine, deceased, occupation wheelwright. Alice gave her father's name as Morris Ayres, occupation dealer. They were married at Guildford Register Office and the witnesses were G. Goodridge and Ellen Goodridge. Only the witnesses could sign their names.

Charles George Walker, aged 22 years, occupation labourer, married Mary Ann Pudvine, aged 22 years, no occupation, on 31st December 1882. Charles gave his address as Milk House Gate and Mary Ann as the Parish of St Nicholas, Guildford. Charles gave his father's name as Charles Walker, a labourer, and Mary Ann gave her father's name as Frederick Pudwine, a labourer. I now know that Frederick is my three times great grandfather and it feels great. I am now confused about the Mary Walker on the 1881 Census as I can find no other record of Mary Pudwine. Perhaps this is her but she preferred the name Walker, but at least I know that Mary Ann and Mary are the same person.

Deaths

Harriett Pudwine died on 20 February 1847, aged 39 years. The cause of death was typhus for 80 days and diarrhoea for six days. Her occupation is noted, as widow of William Pudwine, wheelwright, and present at death was Harriett Downs. What is strange here is that Harriett is a widow but William was still alive in 1847, as he did not die until 1849. Were they separated? Maybe William had been ill for a long time and Harriett thought he was already dead? I now know that Thomas and William Pudwine are the same person.

A female Pudvine died on 6 May 1859 aged one day. She was the daughter of Henry Pudvine, occupation agricultural labourer, who was present at her death and signed with his mark. The cause of death was debility from premature birth, seven months. This moved me because I was able to peep into this couple's world with the information I had found on the Newspaper Detectives site and wondered how this spirited couple must have felt at the loss of their daughter.

Alfred Frederick Pudwine died on 6 April 1862 aged five weeks. He was the son of Frederick Pudwine, an agricultural labourer. The cause of death was pneumonia and the informant of the death was E. Lewis at the Union Workhouse, Guildford.

Charlotte Pudvine died on 2 March 1869 aged 18 months, the daughter of Frederick Pudvine, agricultural labourer who was present at her death in Wood Street Village. The cause of death was pneumonia.

Harriet Pudvine died on 4 June 1869 aged 32 years, the wife of Frederick Pudvine, agricultural labourer, who was present at her death in Wood Street Village. Brian and I used to socialise in Wood Street Village pub. The cause of death was tubercular disease of the lungs for five years, bronchitis and premature child birth for four days. Poor Frederick – a child and his wife within three months and poor Harriet – what a dreadful end to her life.

Alice Pudwine died on 1 June 1871 aged eight years, the daughter of Frederick Pudwine, general labourer. The cause of death was pneumonia for sixteen weeks and present at death was E. Lewis of the Union Workhouse, Guildford.

Emily Pudvine died on 3 August 1877 aged 36 years, the wife of Henry Pudwine, a labourer in a flourmill. The cause of death was renal dropsy for three months, seven days, and present at the death was Henry Pudvine, widower of deceased, at the Royal Surrey Hospital. Her age should read 38 going by the information on her marriage certificate or maybe she lied about her age when she got married. I think it's probably an error on the death certificate.

Emma Pudvine died on 9 August 1882 aged 17 years, occupation domestic servant in Albury and cause of death tubercular ulceration of intestines. The informant of the death was Rysling Marsh, the Resident Medical Officer at the Royal Surrey County Hospital.

Maria Pudvine died on 9 May 1895 aged 54 years in Queens Road, Guildford, the wife of Frederick Pudvine, a farm labourer. Present at the death was Emma Jane Jones. The cause of death was phthisis haemorrhage one day and syncope.

Ada Pudvine died on 22 December 1900 aged 17 years, occupation general servant (domestic), of Margate. Ada was the daughter of Frederick and his second wife Maria and was born in 1883. The cause of death was caries (the decay or death of a bone producing a chronic inflammation that forms an abscess that burrows through soft tissue or opens externally) and cervical vertebral scrofulous paralysis. (Scrofula is a generally hereditary constitutional disease, which manifests as an enlargement and cheesy degeneration of the lymphatic glands, particularly those of the neck, which is tubercular in character. Scrofula was also known as the King's curse or malady during the reigns of Henry VIII and Elizabeth I.) The informant of the death was Samuel Gerrard Master of the Union Workhouse in Minster in the county of Kent. What was Ada doing in Margate? It's such a long way from Guildford, and how sad that she died alone. Maybe there are relatives living in this area! Maybe she was sent to work there for her health! There appears to be a lot of tubercular related disease in my family's heritage. I wonder if that explains why I had a natural defence against TB and did not have to be immunised?

Frederick Pudvine died on 25 September 1906, aged 76 years, a farm labourer from Ockham in Surrey. Frederick died of senile decay at Guildford Workhouse. Frederick's christening record gives a date of 1833, making him only 73 years of age. For some reason in his early 20s Frederick aged himself by three years.

Alice Pudvine died on 22 October 1914 aged 71 years and was the wife of Henry Pudvine, a hawker of Sparrow Row, Valley End, Chobham, Surrey. The cause of death was senility and heart failure, and her son-in-law E. H. Copeland from Upper Holloway was present at her death. Sparrow Row in Chobham still exists and is about five miles from where we live now.

The final death was for Henry Pudvine on 17 March 1916, aged 87 years. His occupation was given as hawker and he was now living in Sunnycote, West End, Chobham. The cause of death was influenza for three days and heart failure. Present at his death was E. M. Dew, the occupier of Sunnycote. His age was given as 87 years but he was only 82 years – maybe he felt like he was 87 years!

What I learned

◆ The marriage certificates for some of William and Harriet's children now confirm that my four times great grandfather is called William and not Thomas.

◆ Ordering Pudvine certificates from districts other than Guildford was a risk worth taking as with Lewis and Ada.

- Later in life William and Harriet must have been parted, as at Harriet's death she believed she was already a widow but William was still living – maybe in the workhouse where he died.
- An ancestor's given age can vary greatly on different sources such as birth, marriage, death, christening or Census records. It does not mean you have the wrong ancestor, it just means you need to verify your information with more sources.
- I was now learning about the medical history of my own family.
- You can never ask too many questions too many times about family memories.
- Blanket searches for unusual family names are worth the time and effort.

I never thought I would say this but my family tree is now too large to show on one page so to keep you up to date I have split my recent finds into two trees (see figures 7.2 and 7.3).

My first visit to the Surrey History Centre

I had previously spoken to Jane at the Surrey History Centre in Woking regarding the work she and her colleagues carried out on my behalf; she recommended a visit to the centre. The Surrey History Centre (SHC) does not hold records of births, marriages and deaths except for the years from 1900 to 1920 for Surrey but they do hold parish records, Census, old newspapers and much more. I did not know this before I went to the Centre (see www.surreycc.gov.uk/surreyhistoryservice.)

During this month I made a couple of visits to the SHC to search Census records for Surrey. The advice I was given by the society is the correct advice and that is to work backwards when researching family history. As an inexperienced researcher who had gone my own way, with surprising success, I already had lots of clues from the certificates I had obtained and wanted to look for specific information. You also have to remember that having family names such as Pudvine, Pudwine or Marelli meant my blanket searches proved very successful. However, this would not have been right for the Walkers or Reynolds, for instance, as there are thousands of them. There will be times when you cannot go any further back and your only option is to go sideways or forwards.

7.2 Direct decendants of William Pudwine

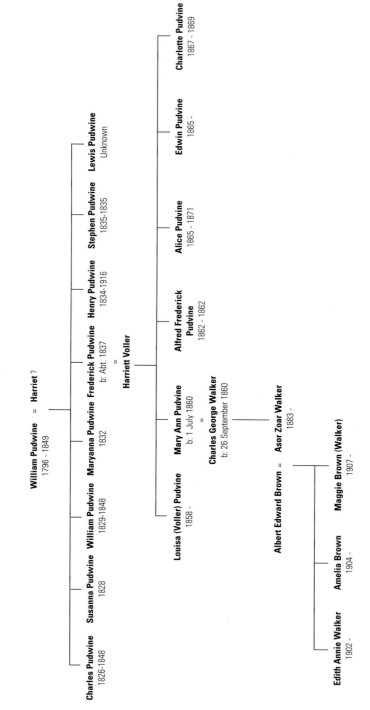

7.3 Ancestors of Asor Zoar Walker

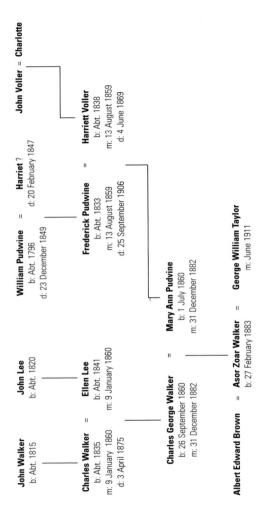

John Voller = **Charlotte**

William Pudwine = **Harriet ?**
b: Abt. 1796   d: 20 February 1847
d: 23 December 1849

Harriett Voller
b: Abt. 1838
m: 13 August 1859
d: 4 June 1869

Frederick Pudwine =
b: Abt. 1833
m: 13 August 1859
d: 25 September 1906

John Lee
b: Abt. 1820

Mary Ann Pudvine
b: 1 July 1860
m: 31 December 1882

John Walker
b: Abt. 1815

Ellen Lee
b: Abt. 1841
m: 9 January 1860

George William Taylor
m: June 1911

Charles Walker =
b: Abt. 1835
m: 9 January 1860
d: 3 April 1875

Charles George Walker =
b: 26 September 1860
m: 31 December 1882

Albert Edward Brown = **Asor Zoar Walker** =
b: 27 February 1883

My first stop was the 1841 Census for Albury and the surrounding area. This is what I found:

◆ William Podevin *(that's a new spelling)*, aged 40 years, occupation strangely given as J. Wheelis – maybe it means the person he worked for. The 1841 Census does not give as much information as later Censuses but there was a (Y) for yes to signify born in same county. I now have conflicting dates of birth for William: the 1841 Census indicates he was born *circa* 1801 and his death certificate indicates he was born *circa* 1796. (But as we know the 1841 Census rounds the birth date down to the nearest five-year mark, so he could have been 44 years of age making his date of birth 1797, near enough matching my earlier estimation that he was born *circa* 1796.)

◆ Harriett Podevin, wife, aged 33 years of no occupation, born in Surrey. (It's strange that Harriett's age is not rounded down.)

◆ Susannah Podevin, aged 13 years, of no occupation, born in Surrey.

◆ William Podevin, aged 12 years, of no occupation, born in Surrey.

◆ Mary Podevin, aged 10 years, of no occupation, born in Surrey.

◆ Frederick Podevin, aged eight years, of no occupation, born in Surrey – so he was born in 1833.

◆ Henry Podevin, aged seven, born in Surrey.

◆ Edward Podevin, aged four born in Surrey.

◆ Elizabeth Podevin aged five weeks, born in Surrey.

This was great news as all those children I had found on the FamilySearch listing for Thomas and Harriett are in fact the children of William and Harriet, my five time great grandparents. The spelling of the name Podevin is of most interest to me at this point.

One of the children that should have been there was Charles who died in 1848 so I kept looking and found:

◆ Charles Pudvine, aged 15, occupation MS (male servant or man servant), born in Surrey; he was working for Ann Ansell, a publican in Albury Village.

I decided to keep searching for other possible family members and found William Voller, his wife Charlotte Voller and their children, John Voller and Sarah Voller. What I needed was John and Charlotte Voller who were the parents of Harriet Voller, Frederick Pudvine's first wife – they could be related though.

I had been at the SHC for several hours and was completely overwhelmed by the amount of searching I had to do. Looking around for inspiration I noticed some cabinets that held film of old newspapers and was told it was the *Surrey Advertiser*. I explained the information I had from the Newspaper Detectives site and was directed to the film I required. Call it luck but, because I had no idea what information to take with me that day, I took everything related to my Surrey ancestors, including a printout of the index for the *Surrey Advertiser* in 1866 taken from the Newspaper Detectives website.

It did not take me long to find the right dates but I had to trawl carefully through the whole newspaper for each article to find what I was looking for. Even though I had the dates of the story, the name Pudwine and the name of the newspaper I could not quite believe I was going to find such personal historic data and my heart was hammering. Sure enough in the newspaper dated 21 April 1866 was a wonderful story about my three times great uncle Henry and his wife Emily. It read:

A Wife and a Policeman – At the Borough Branch, on Monday last, before Messrs. J. Weale and H. A. Adams, *Emily Pudwine* was charged with having committed an assault on P.C. Chatt, while in the execution of his duty. The facts of the case are rather amusing. It appears that on Friday, the 6th inst., about six o'clock in the evening, the defendant's husband and another man were drunk in the High Street. P. C. Chatt, who chanced to come up at the time, ordered the men to 'move on;' but Pudwine refused to do so. The police constable then proceeded to arrest Pudwine, who, however, resisted violently. His resistance became the more daring and violent when he espied his wife turning the corner with an air of 'deep defiance'. When she saw her better half 'chuckled,' she 'flew at' the constable. Another constable (Castleman) who was coming up behind, 'flew at' her, and a mêlée ensued, greatly to the amusement of bystanders, who encouraged the wife in the attack she made. 'Handfuls' of hair, as it was stated, were pulled off the police-constable's head. It required five stalwart members of the force to appease the quarrel. The defendant now denied the entire charge against her, and with tears asserted it was all a 'big lie'. The Bench fined the defendant 20s., or twenty-one days' imprisonment. Some sympathising females present paid the fine.

This was incredible and I had to stop myself from calling out to everyone in the centre saying, 'look what I've found, come and see, everyone, it's amazing'. I still had another story to find but I was twitching to get outside and phone Mum, Brian, Auntie Shirley, my sisters, my brothers, my friends – anyone who would listen! Such luck, such a find and no one to share the moment with!

I returned to look for the second story that was a little more serious, but not much and as far as I was concerned a total miscarriage of justice. Well maybe not!

BOROUGH BENCH – Monday
(Before the Mayor and Mr. Wheale)

AN OLD OFFENCE – A man rejoicing in the peculiar name of Pudwine was charged with being drunk and disorderly. P.C. Northgayle deposed that almost ten o'clock on Saturday night he was going through Stoke-fields when he met the prisoner who was drunk and shouting. He cautioned him and told him to go home, but prisoner refused. Witness then took him into custody but had some difficulty in getting him to the station, as prisoner, who was a powerful man, threw him twice. The prisoner denied that he was drunk, and said he was going along quietly when he was interrogated by the policeman. The latter caught hold of him in the mouth when prisoner gave him a push, and that was what took place between them. The prisoner was fined 10s., and in default was committed for fourteen days.

Was I just the luckiest family historian alive – could this really belong to my family! Is there a God, yes there is and with respect 'Thank God' for the Emilys and Henrys of this world. With copy in hand I raced once more to the car and my phone.

When I thought I might burst with excitement I was told incredibly that I could view the 1901 Census on microfiche at the Centre. Who was alive then and living in Surrey? I scanned my documents. There was my grandfather Harry on Mum's side who was living in Epsom, and also Asor Zora who gave birth to her daughter Edith in Knaphill. I thought it might be interesting to see if I could find out who had lived in the house in Knaphill where Edith was born as they could be related. I began my search of Epsom and this is what I found:

◆ Living in Epsom was Robert Reynolds, head of household, aged 40 years, occupation engine driver – stationary. There was someone else in the family that had this job, but what was most interesting was it gave his place of birth as Bow, London, not Epsom. My great grandfather was born within the sound of Bow Bells, which perhaps explains why my grandfather's accent was more Cockney than Surrey, and there was me, a Liverpool lass!

◆ There was Eliza Reynolds, wife, aged 39 years, no occupation, born in Banstead, Surrey.

◆ There were Ada aged ten born in Dorking, Edith aged eight, Annie aged six, Lilian aged four (was Mum named after her aunt?), Edgar R. aged two and Harry W. aged one month. The latter was my grandfather – all born in Epsom. (I must look at the 1891 Census for the Dorking area at some point.)

When trying to find your local family history establishments you can source information on the web via Genuki or Cyndi's List or type in search criteria on the address line such as 'family history Devon.' Failing that you could phone your local library and ask for advice - they may have useful facilities to offer or at least be able to point you in the right direction.

My next find was not at all what I expected. I looked up the address for Asor Zora in Knaphill hoping to find a relative or perhaps that it was a home for unmarried mothers as this is where Asor Zora's first child Edith would be born the following year. This is what I found:

◆ Charles G. Walker, head, aged 40, occupation stoker at asylum, born in Guildford;
◆ Mary Ann Walker, wife, aged 40, no occupation, born in Worplesdon;
◆ Asor Zora Walker, daughter, aged 18, no occupation, born in Guildford;

- Charles G. Walker, son, aged 16, labourer on railway, born in Woking District;
- Frederick Walker, son, aged 14;
- Nellie Walker, daughter, aged 12;
- Amelia Walker, daughter, aged nine;
- Albert Walker, son, aged seven;
- Alfred Walker, son, aged four;
- Sydney Walker, son, aged one;
- The last six children were born in the Woking District.

So Asar Zora was living at home with her parents when Edith was born. Had I not been curious to know who was living at the address on Edith's birth certificate I might not have found this information for quite some time.

What amazes me about discovering my ancestors in my local area is that I may have met a descendant of an ancestor and not known it. I've had a horrible thought – I could have dated one of them prior to meeting Brian! I hope not. I wonder how many times that happens in families with lost generations?

Census and certificates working together

With the address I had on Edith Walker's birth certificate I was able to locate her whole family without much effort on the 1901 Census for Surrey on microfiche. Without this information I would never have thought to search the Knaphill area, although I probably would have found them at a later date with the 1901 Census online as you can search this Census by name.

Now I have the above Census information for the Walker family in Knaphill I should be able to easily source birth certificates for all Asar Zora's siblings. Without this Census information my chances of locating other children of Charles and Mary Ann among the thousands of Walkers in the Birth Registers would have been near impossible and probably extremely expensive, as I would have first looked at the Guildford district.

I highly recommend searching the Census first for ancestors with common names such as Walker if you have a district where you know your ancestors were based. Although searching the Census could potentially take many hours, days or weeks, it is the less expensive option to ordering certificates at random in the hope of striking lucky!

About this time I decided to write to the Pudvine that my friend Sue had found for me giving him a brief outline of what I had found and asking if the information meant anything to him. I had a phone call back to say he was thrilled to receive my letter, as he believed he was the only living Pudvine descendant. We chatted about all I knew and tried to find some connection. He said he believed his grandfather or great grandfather lived in London and was called George and married someone called Frances. Sadly it meant nothing to me, as I only knew of Lewis who had lived in London.

I decided to head to the FRC to try to find George Walker, the other child of Asor Zora, to complete this part of the family. My thinking now was that he could have been born elsewhere. I found two possible birth certificates, one for George Albert Walker born in Guildford in1902 and one for Charles George Walker in 1904 – they were both incorrect. I spent a lot of time looking for possibilities but who knows what surname George was born under? It could have been Walker or Brown, or was there another man in Asor Zora's life?

I had taught myself to avoid depressing disappointment when searching for the impossible ancestor by always having information with me about a certainty. Then I would not feel that I had wasted my day by going home empty handed. I decided to find another of Charles and Ellen Walker's children and I also looked for the birth of Charlotte Pudvine who as yet I had not found.

The certificates arrive

Amelia Caroline Walker was born on 12 January 1892 in Jay's Cottage, Knaphill. She was the daughter of Charles George Walker, a labourer (general) at Brookwood Asylum, and Mary Ann Walker, formerly Pudvine.

Charlotte Pudvine was born on 7 July 1867 in Wood Street, Worplesdon, daughter of Frederick Pudvine, an agricultural labourer, and Harriett Pudvine, formerly Voller.

What I have learned

◆ Visiting other establishments such as the Surrey History Centre, as some of my ancestors come from Surrey, can prove extremely beneficial, especially with the newspaper archive I found.

◆ At some point I would need to search the 1891 Census in Dorking for my grandfather Robert Reynolds as the 1901 Census told me his eldest child was born there ten years previously. I would never have looked in Dorking without this valuable piece of information.

◆ Without a specific address for an ancestor searching the Census can be a laborious task, but is not as expensive as randomly ordering incorrect certificates.

◆ Being inquisitive helps. Had I not been curious to look up the address on Edith Walker's, Maggie's sister's, birth certificate I would not have found the whole family of my three times great grandparents Charles and Ellen Walker for quite some time.

◆ It is worth contacting strangers if you think that a possible family link exists. I have always had a positive response even if there is no link and the contacts I have made have always been interested in the subject of family history.

I do not take any of the information I have found lightly. I am so lucky, but again I find my irritation building as I cannot find any information about the William Pudvine, Pudwine or Podevin birth. I even thought about going to a psychic to try to contact him personally!

8 Looking for William (May 2002)

I wanted to find out more about William Pudwine or Podevin but a further search on the FamilySearch site gave me only one possibility, for a William Potvine christened on 16 May 1793 in Saint Mary Magdalene, Canterbury, Kent.

Disappointed I headed back to the Surrey History Centre to search the Census.

When visiting establishments such as the SHC to view records it is advisable to phone first and check if you need to reserve film or fiche viewers, if there is an entrance fee and what facilities they have. You could be there many hours and you may need to take with you a packed lunch and drinks if there are no facilities.

Many record extracts can now be viewed on line: www.surreycc.gov.uk/surreyhistorycentre and select Search for Archives of Books.

By 1851 both William Pudwine and his wife Harriet were dead and I wondered what had happened to the younger children. I searched all the villages surrounding Guildford and eventually found them in the 1851 Census in Hambledon Union Workhouse.

Henry Podevine (again the strange spelling of the surname, as if it wasn't strange enough already) was sixteen years of age, an agricultural labourer born in Albury. Also with him was Edward aged fifteen, Mary aged twenty, Ann aged eleven and excitingly, Lewis aged six, the latter two born in Bramley. This was the second mention of Lewis after finding his marriage certificate with a London address. I was so pleased I had followed my instincts on this one.

With the above success I decided to search the Worplesdon area as there were several Pudwine/Pudvine children born there.

My next find was equally thrilling although not what I was looking for. I at last found John and Charlotte Voller. John was a farm labourer aged 53 and Charlotte 46 years of age both born in Worplesdon. With them was Charles aged sixteen years and Emily aged twelve years, both born in Worplesdon. Emily was obviously Henry's wife. There was also Albert aged seven years and Henry aged five years, both born in Stoke near Guildford where this Census was taken. Also living in the same house was James Marsh aged 76 years, father-in-law. Remarkably I had stumbled across another generation. This meant that Charlotte Voller was formerly Charlotte Marsh. Also Charles Voller was a witness at my three times great grandfather Frederick's marriage to Harriet which has now convinced me that Harriet and Emily Voller were sisters who married Pudwine or Pudvine brothers.

I also fell across two families called Bonsey, a name that was familiar to me, and took copies of these pages only to find when I got home and checked through my records that I had found Richard Bonsey who would marry William and Harriet's daughter Susanna later that year. The family consisted of Richard Bonsey, head, aged 50, occupation shoemaker, Mary Bonsey his wife, aged 56, and Richard Bonsey, their son aged 22, occupation railway labourer. Also living in the house were Benjamin aged 19 and John aged 16. The other family also had two family members listed by the name of Benjamin so I decided to hold onto this information for a later date.

Going back to William Pudwine I was now beginning to think that the spelling of the name Pudwine or Pudvine was taken from the pronunciation rather than knowledge of how it was spelt, as there were several derivatives of the family name. Also, whenever I searched for Pudwine on FamilySearch, a whole variety of names appeared from Potvin and Potvain to Pudwine, Poitevin and Podevin, the latter proving to be of the most interest with the other evidence I had collected. There was nothing about William's birth or christening. I was beginning to get frustrated again because if I could not find details of his birth then I would not be able to trace this line any further!

Back at home on the 1881 Census, as I had not found Henry Pudwine I decided to look for his second wife Alice Bristow. I found her living in

Castle Street, Guildford, a widow aged 42 born in Adlow, Kent, and with her were two daughters Ellen aged six years and Mary aged three years both born in Guildford. A quick check of the marriage certificate of Alice and Henry told me they married later that same year so I searched the neighbourhood. To my utter delight I found Henry Pudwine recorded as Henry Indwine. I knew it was my Henry because he was a widower who was born in Wonersh, the same district as Albury, and also because, amusingly, he was living in the Rising Sun public house – quite fitting as he appeared to like a drink.

On the same Census by trawling through the National Index of Surnames I also found Lewis Pudwine/vine in London. He was listed under the name Lewis Rudine, aged 33, born in Bramley, Surrey. With him was his wife Grace Rudine aged 32 and her sister Christina Fergusson. Finding Grace's sister with the same surname as her own maiden name confirmed my find was correct. I looked up the address where Lewis was living at the time of his marriage two years previously at 19 Belgrave Square. Living at that address in 1881 was William Ernest Duncombe, Peer of Parliament and Mabel Molet (Countess) Forenshaw along with four children, one of whom was a Lieutenant in the Scots Guards. How very real this made Lewis to me.

A further search revealed Ann Rose, nee Pudwine, who had married Henry Rose. They were living in Pirbright, another village local to us where we have socialised, and also right next to Brookwood Cemetery where Martino Marelli and son Martin are buried. They are listed as Henry Rose aged 42, an agricultural labourer, his wife Annie Rose (Ann) aged 41 and their children William aged 13, Lizzie aged 11, Lillian (*sic*) aged five and Harrey (*sic*) aged two.

Another search on FamilySearch playing with the spelling of the surname Pudwine brought me the christening record of Ann Podavine, daughter of William and Harriet Podavine. With another proof of birth recording William as the father, I now thought I should concentrate on looking for William Pudwine rather than Thomas Pudwine. If I had no luck searching for him I would then concentrate on the Christian name of Thomas or both. But how do I find William?

8.1a Descendants of James Marsh to Mary Ann Pudvine

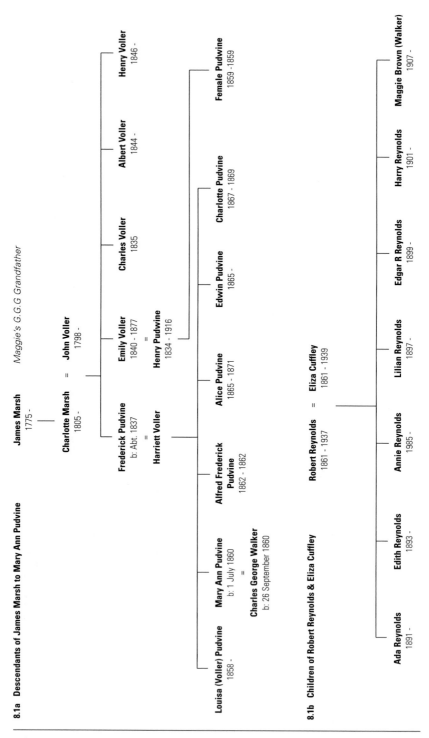

James Marsh
1775 -

Maggie's G.G.G Grandfather

Charlotte Marsh   =   **John Voller**
1805 -   1798 -

Frederick Pudvine   **Emily Voller**   **Charles Voller**   **Albert Voller**   **Henry Voller**
b: Abt. 1837   1840 - 1877   1835   1844 -   1846 -
                              =
Harriett Voller   **Henry Pudwine**
                         1834 - 1916

Alfred Frederick   **Alice Pudvine**   **Edwin Pudvine**   **Charlotte Pudvine**   **Female Pudwine**
Pudvine   1865 - 1871   1865 -   1867 - 1869   1859 -1859
1862 - 1862

Louisa (Voller) Pudvine   **Mary Ann Pudvine**
1858 -   b: 1 July 1860
                                     =
                                 Charles George Walker
                                 b: 26 September 1860

8.1b Children of Robert Reynolds & Eliza Cuffley

Robert Reynolds   =   **Eliza Cuffley**
1861 - 1937   1861 - 1939

Ada Reynolds   **Edith Reynolds**   **Annie Reynolds**   **Lilian Reynolds**   **Edgar R Reynolds**   **Harry Reynolds**   **Maggie Brown (Walker)**
1891 -   1893 -   1985 -   1897 -   1899 -   1901 -   1907 -

8.2a Children of William Pudwine

Maggie's G.G.
Grandfather

William Pudwine = Harriet ?
1796 - 1849

Charles Pudwine
1826-1848

Susanna
Pudwine
1828
=
Richard Bonsey

William
Pudwine
1829-1848

Maryanna
Pudwine
1832

Frederick Pudwine
b: Abt. 1837
=
(1) Harriett Voller
1838–1869
(2) Maria Webber
1848–1895

Henry Pudwine
1834-1916
=
(1) Emily Voller
1840-1877
(2) Alice Bristow
1838–1914

Stephen
Pudwine
1835-1835

Edward Pudwine
1837–

Elizabeth
Pudwine
1841–

Lewis Pudwine
=
Grace Ferguson

8.2b Children of Charles George Walker & Mary Ann Pudvine

Maggie's Grandparents

Charles George Walker = Mary Ann Pudvine
1860 -   1860 -

Asor Zoar Walker
1883 -
=
(1) Albert Edward Brown
(2) George William Taylor

Charles G
Walker
1885 -

Frederick Walker
1887 -

Nellie Walker
1889 -

Amelia Walker
1892 -

Albert Walker
1894 -

Alfred Walker
1897 -

Sydney Walker
1900 -

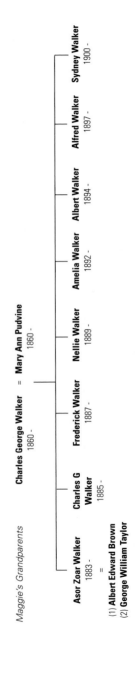

8.3 Descendants of Frederick Pudwine Maggie's Great Grandfather

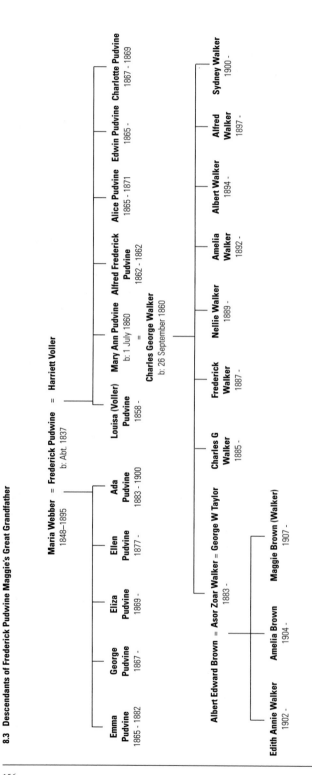

To keep you in the picture but to make things simple I have split the family trees into groups (see figures 8.1, 8.2 and 8.3).

I decided to return to the Surrey History Centre to find parish records on film for some of the Pudwine children of William (Thomas) and Harriet Pudwine.

Parish records viewed on film at the Surrey History Centre, and other similar establishments, can be photocopied for your own records.

1. The first I found was for Susanna Pudwine dated 1828, daughter of Thomas and Harriet, the occupation of Thomas being papermaker (occupational information is not given on the FamilySearch site). This disappointed me because I wanted Thomas to have been an input error on FamilySearch. Also the occupation of papermaker was a little disconcerting.

2. William Pudwine was next, dated 1829, son of William and Harriet. The occupation given for William was wheeler.

3. Mary Annie Pudwine was next, dated 1832. On FamilySearch her Christian name is Maryanne, parents Thomas and Harriet, the occupation of Thomas being wheeler.

4. Next was Frederick Pudwine, dated 1833, my three times great grandfather, parents Thomas and Harriet, the occupation of Thomas being wheeler (see figure 8.4). Frederick stated on his marriage certificate

8.4 Parish record for Frederick Pudwine

that his father was William, so this had to be an error in the parish register. William and Thomas must be the same person. Perhaps his name was Thomas William or William Thomas.

5. Next was Henry Pudwine, dated 1834; his parents and the occupation of his father were the same as above.

6. I also found Stephen dated 1835 with parents and occupation of father the same as above. As I had a death record for a Stephanie dated 25 September 1835 from the National Burial Index I decided to check burials and found only Stephen for this date, so the National Burial Index is a misprint.

7. Finally I looked up Ann Podavine dated 1841. This also turned out to be a misprint on FamilySearch – it should have been Ann Podevin, the other spelling of Pudwine again. She was the daughter of William and Harriet Podevin of Bramley, the occupation of William this time being millwright.

I was so pleased I had the above parish records and also the Census records because, although they are only copies, to me they are the real thing and a real piece of my family history. I cannot explain the pleasure in seeing the writing of the person responsible for recording this information in parish records or looking at the details of who else is recorded on the same page, wondering if my ancestors and these other families knew each other.

Another search of the Census looking at the villages surrounding Guildford brought me the following:

1861 – Worplesdon

- Frederick Pudwine, head, aged 26, occupation shepherd, born in Albury;
- Harriet Pudwine, wife, aged 28 years, born in Worplesdon;
- Louisa Voller, daughter, aged three years, born in Stoke;
- Mary Pudwine, daughter, aged nine months, born in Worplesdon;
- John Voller, father, widower, aged 64 years, occupation agricultural labourer, born in Worplesdon.

1871 – Guildford Workhouse

- John Voller, inmate, widower, aged 74 years, agricultural labourer born in Worplesdon;
- Frederick Pudwine, inmate, widower, aged 35 years, agricultural labourer born in Albury;
- Louisa Pudwine (taken the Surname of her stepfather), inmate, aged 13, scholar, born in Worplesdon;

- Mary Ann Pudwine, (Asor Zoar's mother), inmate, aged 11, scholar, born in Worplesdon;
- Alice Pudwine, inmate, aged eight, scholar, born in Worplesdon;
- All the above are resident in Guildford Workhouse.

(Frederick had lost his first wife, Harriet, at this stage and I assume that his youngest children were staying with relatives.)

I also found another entry for Edward Pudwine, aged 34, a labourer living in lodgings in Guildford (William and Harriet's son).

1881

Although I already had the 1881 Census records on CD I decided to obtain copies of the original records of the following:

- Frederick and his second wife Maria and children who were living in Albury;
- Ellen Walker and family living in Milk House Gate;
- Alice Bristow, second wife of Henry Pudwine, living in Castle Street, Guildford;
- Henry Pudwine also living in the Rising Sun Pub in Castle Street, Guildford (Henry is spelt Indwine on the CD-ROM version of the 1881 Census, but still, I'm not complaining).

1901

I found Henry Pudwine, aged 67, and Alice Pudwine aged 57, living in Sparrow Row, Chobham. Henry's occupation was given as agricultural labourer.

Census returns can be purchased for some areas of the country on CD-Rom from S&N Genealogy Supplies by telephone on 01722 716121 or via their websites www.genealogysupplies.com or www.britishdataarchive.com or www.thegenealogist.co.uk. For instance, I have purchased the 1861, 1871 and 1891 Censuses for London to search for a number of family members for whom I did not have addresses, only districts. To do this on film at the FRC would have taken many months, perhaps years, because of the amount of searching required. For me the cost of the Censuses outweighed the cost of travelling back and forth to London. These census are scanned copies of originals and are quite difficult to read although you can zoom in for an enlarged view on your PC. Census records can now be viewed online via subscription on the following websites: www.ancestry.co.uk – all census years, and www.findmypast.com – some census years.

Another visit to the FRC

The first death certificate was for Charlotte Voller dated 20 March 1857, aged 50 years, wife of John Voller, an agricultural labourer. The cause of death was scrofula for fifteen years and dropsy for seven days. Scrofula is hereditary and although Ada, Frederick's daughter, died of the same complaint she is not the granddaughter of Charlotte because she is the child of Frederick's second wife Maria, so I have to assume this complaint was common and in more than one branch of my family. Hannah Whale was present at the death.

The next death is for Maria Pudvine dated 24 January 1880, aged five years. I nearly didn't get this certificate because it was registered in Leicester. It states she is the daughter of Frederick Pudvine, a labourer. The cause of death was pneumonia and the informant of death was E. Dickinsson (*sic*), Matron of Leicester Union Workhouse. I can only assume that Frederick moved to this area to find work.

I found another death for a Frederick George Pudvine in Bromley, Kent, dated 2 September 1904 aged three months. He was the son of Helen Pudvine, spinster and domestic servant. The cause of death was syncope from tubercular desease of the heart from natural causes. Under informant it stated the certificate was received from J. Powell, Coroner of Kent, and the inquest was held 5 September 1904. As yet I have not found a connection with my family but my instincts tell me there could be eventually.

The final death certificate was for Lewis Pudwine dated 15 December 1907, aged 64 years. The occupation was given as caretaker of mansion, and the cause of death as pneumonia and heart disease. Present at the death was Gertrude Pudvine, his daughter. Lewis died in Stamford House, Newmarket.

I moved to Births to carry out a blanket search of the name Pudwine but as I had not found the birth certificate for Lewis I decided to look under variations of the spelling of the surname. I found Lewis under the surname of Podavin dated 10 March 1843, son of William Podavin, a wheelwright, and Harriott Podavin, formerly Saunders. Lewis was registered in Hambledon, Cranley (*sic*) but William's address is Bramley. Lewis is not recorded in the FamilySearch records. Later this month I would find a record at the Surrey History Centre of Lewis Pudevine baptised on 27 March 1843, parents William and Harriet, occupation of father, wheelwright.

The next birth I found was a complete surprise - it was for a Jane Pudvine dated 22 August 1846. Jane was the daughter of William Pudwine, wheelwright, but the mother is recorded as Sarah Pudwine, formerly Saunders, and hysterically the informant of the birth is Harriett Pudwine, mother. Surely the registrar must have noticed he had two differently named mothers on the same certificate? I was delighted with this extra find but also because I had further confirmation that Harriet was previously a Saunders or Sanders.

A birth for a Henry Pudwin in North Aylesford, Kent, dated 19 February 1847 is a bit of a mystery. Henry is the son of Richard Pudwin and Ann Pudwin, formerly Decan. I ordered this certificate because of the Christian name and also because the surname was so close to Pudwine, although at this moment I couldn't find any family connection.

I found the birth certificate for Alfred Frederick Pudwine dated 25 February 1862, one for Alice Pudvine dated 3 May 1863 and one for Emma Pudvine dated 25 August 1865, all children of Frederick and Harriet Pudvine.

The next birth was for a Maria Pudvine born in Richmond, Surrey, on 31 October 1874. Maria is the daughter of Frederick Pudvine and his second wife Maria Pudvine, formerly Webber. She was born in Richmond Workhouse. So I now know that Frederick lived in Richmond in 1874 and Leicester in 1880.

I found two other children from the marriage of Maria and Frederick, one for Ellen Pudvine born in Hambledon on 6 April 1877 and one for Frederick Pudvine born in Croydon on 8 June 1879. Both children were born in the workhouse. So Frederick had now also lived in Croydon.

During a relatively short space of time Frederick had lived in Guildford in 1871, Richmond in 1874, Hambledon, Surrey in 1877, Croydon, Surrey in 1879, Leicester in 1880 and back to Albury in 1881. This gave me a strong reason to believe that Frederick must have been working with a travelling agricultural labouring gang. (I had purchased a couple of books about rural life in Surrey during the nineteenth century that explained about labouring gangs.)

The next certificate was for Frederick George Pudvine born on 2 June 1904, son of Helen Pudvine of Kent whose death certificate I had also acquired, and felt that a connection might be established one day.

Finally were the certificates for two daughters of Lewis Pudvine. Edith Pudvine was born on 24 December 1881 and Gertrude on 25 September 1883. Both were daughters of Lewis and Grace Pudvine, formerly Fergusson. The occupation of Lewis is given as lodging house keeper in Paddington, London.

My friend Sue was interested, as I was, that Lewis Pudvine had died in Newmarket because there had been no mention of this district previously. We both searched the Internet for information about Stamford House. (We are lucky that Wendy our boss allows us to use this facility at work, and we try not to take advantage of her generosity.) Sadly we could not find anything although Sue did find a site called Newmarket Local History Society (www.wood-ditton.org.uk/newmarketlhs.htm) and sent an e-mail explaining about Lewis Pudvine. Below is part of the information we received back from Rod Vincent, the recorder for the website taking queries and comments:

> Stamford House was the middle house of three occupied by Lady Stamford. One of the other houses was lived in by Lady Cardigan and all the three houses made up the original Panton's House a substantial mansion owned by Thomas Panton who was the 'Keeper of the King's Running Horses' for George II. After he died in the early 19th century the house went to a notorious gambler called William Crockford and after his death the mansion was divided up into three houses.

I searched the net for a William Crockford and on www.thegoodgamblingguide.co.uk website below is an edited version of what I found. Although there is no mention of Stamford House or Newmarket in this particular bit of information it is still interesting.

William Crockford b. 1771 – d. 29 May 1844 London

William was founder and proprietor of the most famous English gambling establishment. His career was remarkable from start to finish. He had been a fishmonger of Fleet Street with a sideline in bookmaking and such small-scale swindles as the three-card trick. In 1816 he bought a quarter-share in a gambling tavern in St James's, but Crockford realised that this tavern could only have limited success. So after winning a large sum of money – £100,000, according to one story – either at cards or from running his gambling club, in 1827 he built a luxuriously decorated gambling house at 50 St James's Street in London. This was an exclusive membership club and almost every English celebrity from the Duke of Wellington down frequented his establishment. Hazard was the favourite game at the club and large sums changed hands. Crockford retired in 1840 with about £1,200,000 but he subsequently lost most of this in unlucky speculations. His establishment eventually became know as the Devonshire Club.

While at the FRC during the month of May I trawled unsuccessfully for the marriage certificate of Frederick Pudvine to Maria Webber. Thinking that as his eldest daughter Maria had been born in Richmond he might have been married there I wrote to the Register Office there and asked for a search to be carried out. Surprisingly they were unable to search for a marriage for me because I could not supply the name of the building in which the marriage took place. They suggested I try the FRC even though I had explained I had already searched there.

Ordering certificates and searches from your local Register Office

Because of time constraints I approached the Register Office in Guildford and asked them to carry out searches on my behalf. After an initial phone call to establish what service was available, I wrote to them enclosing an SAE with the relevant information and a separate cheque for each certificate. What is excellent about applying for certificates locally is that if they do not find a particular individual your cheque or cheques will be returned to you in full.

I carried out more searches on FamilySearch and found a possible birth record for William Pudwine although I was not happy about the date. It was for William Alexander Parker Podevin born on 2 January 1806 to parents Joseph and Ann Podevin. However, I did find an interesting marriage. It was for William Podevin and Harriet Saunders dated 3 April 1826 in Saint Mary, Newington. Up until this date I had only searched in Guildford and the surrounding area.

I was so excited about this and investigated how to go about acquiring a copy of this record in the hope it would give me details of William and Harriet's parents. I found an address for a small branch of the Church of the Latter-Day Saints in Aldershot via the FamilySearch site. After a phone call I visited the church full of hope only to find they would have to order the film with the record I required from America but surprisingly within only a couple of weeks it arrived. Sure enough I found the marriage record but unfortunately no information about either parent. I asked if I could have a copy of the record but they did not have facilities at this site to provide copies.

As I had the name of the church I went onto the Internet and again simply typed in what I was looking for – 'St Mary Newington Church.' To my delight up popped a website and there was also an e-mail address. I e-mailed and asked where the records for births, marriages and deaths were kept and had an almost immediate response giving me the following information:

The London Metropolitan Archives
40 Northampton Road
London EC1R 0HB
Tel: (+44) 020 7332 3820 (Reception)
(+44) 020 7332 3822 (Parish records)
Fax: (+44) 020 7833 9136
E-mail: ask.lma@cityoflondon.gov.uk

8.5 Parish record from St. Mary Newington for the marriage of William Podevin to Harriet Saunders

I e-mailed the above and received a form that would enable me, for a small fee, to order a copy of William and Harriet's marriage record; I received the document a short time later (see figure 8.5).

As you can see witnesses at the marriage were W. and A. Davey and I wondered if one of them might be a relative of William or Harriett. I decided to look for a marriage for William Davey, William being a good bet for the Christian name. I also hoped to establish a link to Albury where William and Harriet came to be living. What I found was that William Davey married Ann Slade on 4 November 1817 in Albury, Surrey. The Daveys had to be part of the reason why William ended up in Albury – perhaps William or Harriet originally came from Albury.

I had a birth date of *circa* 1808 for Harriet from the 1841 Census and her death certificate so I searched FamilySearch for a record of her birth around this date. I found two possible records – one was for the Leatherhead area but the other was for Puttenham, a village on the outskirts of Guildford. The latter was for Harriot Sanders dated 19 July 1807, born in Puttenham, and the other for a Harriot Saunders born in Leatherhead of the same date. Either of these could be my Harriet, but although Puttenham is on the outskirts of Guildford I cannot discount Leatherhead either, it being only a few miles from Albury. In addition, the Harriot from Leatherhead has the correct spelling of the surname.

My feelings on the above information collectively is that Harriet knew the Daveys from her home somewhere in the Guildford area and perhaps went with them to find work in Newington, or maybe they invited her to stay with them. While Harriet was residing in Newington she met William Podevin, married him and they both moved to her local area where he found work in Albury. This is the only theory with a few clues but to me it makes sense.

I also managed to find on FamilySearch a John Voller, christened on 19 June 1831. That had to be the brother of Harriet Voller, Frederick's first wife, as the parents are John and Charlotte Voller.

What I learned

- ◆ When you find an ancestor on a Census return also search around the locality, as you are likely to find other family members.
- ◆ Searching the Census can also produce further generations – as happened with James Marsh, father of Charlotte who married John Voller – another four times great grandfather.
- ◆ You should consider not only variations of spelling where your ancestors are concerned but also origins of surnames as with the strangely spelled surname of Pudwine.

- Researching witnesses at weddings of your ancestors can bring further clues as with the Daveys at William and Harriet's marriage which gave me another link to Albury near Guildford.
- It is always worth e-mailing and asking for help as I did with St Mary's Church.

I now had enough information to convince me that my Pudvine and Pudwine ancestors were descendants of French origin. The surname Podevin in French apparently means 'pot of wine' so again another of Mum's recollections proved correct and we did have French ancestors.

French Ancestors
(June to September 2001)

June 2001

At the beginning of this month I was rereading all the Census records and parish records that I had collected when I noticed on the same page of the record for Frederick Pudwine's baptism, a family of Saunders right above the entry for Frederick. The details were for John Saunders, dated 13 January 1833, son of John and Caroline Saunders of Shalford, Surrey. The father's occupation was papermaker.

This gave me further confidence that Harriet had once lived in the area of Guildford, because when William first moved to Albury his occupation was also papermaker. Maybe a relative of Harriet's found him some work while he was looking for something in his own trade of wheelwright.

A visit to Surrey History Centre resulted in the discovery of the baptism record for John Voller, son of John and Charlotte Voller, dated 19 June 1831, and also a copy of the banns of marriage between John Valler (Voller) and Charlotte Marsh dated 7, 14, and 21 September 1828.

Another search on the FamilySearch site took me back several generations, in some cases as far as 1562. I will have to verify this information at a future date with Surrey History Centre so I will not confuse you any more by listing this exciting but still questionable information.

To search back several generations on FamilySearch:

1. First locate a birth for a known ancestor. This will give you the names of their parents.
2. Next look for details of the parents' marriage which will give you a marriage date.
3. Work out an approximate age at marriage then look for the birth or christening details of the parents. This in turn will give you the names of the next generation of parents and from there go to marriages again and keep going back as far as records exist.

You can then also search for siblings for each marriage by searching the surrounding years of a birth date. However, this could be time-consuming as you will not have Christian names and there could be hundreds of records to view.

Although my latest finds are fascinating I desperately want to source records of more recent ancestors and solve some queries:

◆ I needed details of the birth or christening of William Podevin and who his parents were as I now suspected that William was descended from French origins with possible links to the French Revolution or the Huguenots.
◆ I still had not found birth certificates for Emily or Harriet Voller, Frederick and Henry's wives.
◆ Nor had I found the birth certificate for Thomas Pudwine, son of William and Harriet.
◆ I had not found a marriage certificate for Frederick Pudvine to Maria Webber or for two of their children listed on the 1881 Census as Eliza and George.
◆ I also wanted to find details of my granddad on my father's side of the family; Charles Maloney, born, it is believed, in Liverpool in the 1860s.
◆ Neither had I found Albert Brown, Maggie's father.
◆ Nor had I found the marriage certificate of Albert Brown to Asor Zoar.
◆ I also needed to research more church records for other ancestors and for other clues.

A visit to the FRC brought me two incorrect births for a Charles Maloney and two incorrect Voller births.

I did source the birth certificate for Thomas Podavine dated 1 May 1845, son of William Podavine a wheelwright, and Harriott Podavine, formerly Saunders, born in Hambledon, Surrey. I also found the birth certificate of the daughter of Henry and Emily Pudvine who did not survive and interestingly had the mother listed as Emma Pudvine, formerly Waller, instead of Emily Pudvine, formerly Voller.

So much recorded information is incorrect either due to the illiteracy of the parents who were reliant on the competence of the registrar or because the registrar made errors. I also ordered the birth certificate of the unnamed son of Harriet and Frederick Pudvine who was born four days before his mother died, dated 1 June 1869.

I did not need these last two certificates but felt duty bound not to leave them out.

I tried and tried to find a marriage certificate for Frederick Pudvine to Maria Webber but failed again and again. Back at home I laid out all the information about Frederick and his family I had and established that Eliza and George would have been born prior to the death of Harriet, Frederick's first wife. This meant that either Frederick was having an affair while his wife was ill, which seemed unlikely as he appeared to be a caring man having married Harriet who already had an illegitimate child, or Maria had been married previously, or that she had two illegitimate children. I went back to the FRC to search for a possible first marriage certificate for Maria Webber but could not find one, so I decided to look for George and Eliza under the surname of Webber which brought me the following:

◆ Henry George Webber born in Guildford on 1 October 1867, son of Maria Webber, name of father omitted;

◆ Eliza Webber born in Guildford Workhouse on 13 February 1869, son of Maria Webber, name of father omitted.

So Maria Webber had two children prior to her relationship with Frederick and although they lived together for many years producing children, so far there is no evidence of their marriage.

A search of deaths looking at various spellings of the name Pudwine brought me the following deaths:

◆ Jane Podevine, aged six weeks, dated 5 October 1846, daughter of William Podevine, a wheelwright, and Harriet Podevine, who was present at her death in Saint Mary's Guildford, cause of death being convulsion;

- Thomas Podevine, aged 18 months, dated 20 November 1846, son of William Podevine, a wheelwright, and Harriet Podevine, who was present at his death in Saint Mary's Guildford, cause of death being diarrhoea for 14 days.

As I had the birth certificate for the unnamed son of Frederick and Harriet born four days prior to Harriet's death I ordered the death certificate. He died two days before Harriet on 2 June 1869. The certificate stated this child was one and a half days old, son of Frederick Pudvine, an agricultural labourer, who was also present at his death; the cause of death was given as premature birth at seven months.

I did source the death certificate for John Voller, father of Harriet who was the first wife of Frederick Pudvine: John Voller, dated 29 December 1879, aged 89 years, occupation labourer, cause of death decay of age, informant Master of Union Workhouse. From Census record information John Voller was only *circa* 82 at his death. Still, in the scheme of things he did well to reach that age.

I was beginning to become fractious by the fact I could not find any more information about William Podevin so I called the SoG again looking for inspiration and spoke to a very sympathetic lady who listened attentively to my problem. She suggested I could either search through their records or look for other clues by searching deaths of Podevin in the early years of the FRC indexes. I hadn't thought of that! I might find a brother or sister or even father or mother of William. I also took the opportunity to mention my success in finding Maggie after the advice given and the subsequent visit to the SoG; she was amazed with my result, as my chances of finding her that way were extremely slim.

I found two Podevin deaths in Dover and decided to order these certificates. One of Frederick's daughters died in this area so there could be a family link.

- Henry Podevin, dated 10 December 1840, aged 40 years, occupation Porter, cause of death consumption and present at death Susanna Laurance (*sic*);

- Mary Ann Podwin, dated 2 May 1841, aged seven years, daughter of William Podwin, a labourer, cause of death brain fever, present at death Margaret Fekens.

I felt I was clutching at straws again – only the Christian names held any relevance but the rest of the information was useless.

July 2002

I was out of the country on holiday for two weeks, plus one week prior to going spent getting ready and one week following the holiday trying to undo all the getting ready!

August 2002

I purchased the 1891 Census for Lancashire from S&N Genealogy Supplies and found my dad, Charles Moloney, aged three years, his father Charles, aged 26, and his mother Elizabeth, aged 29. Also listed are my great grandparents, Charles aged 60 born in Liverpool and Bridget aged 50 born in Ireland. There was also my dad's uncle Edward aged 27 also born in Liverpool. (S&N advertise the Census amongst many other products available to help with your research in the popular family history magazines available or on their websites.)

I visited the FRC and looked for the birth certificates for my grandfather, Charles Maloney, born c.1862, and his brother Edward, born a couple of years previously. I ordered two incorrect certificates.

I also searched deaths for Bridget and Charles Moloney/Maloney and ordered one incorrect certificate for Bridget.

On a whim I decided to search for some marriages of Pudwine and found one for George Henry Pudvine, aged 36 years, a bachelor, occupation labourer, to Fanny. George does not give the name of his father.

This confirmed my suspicion that George Henry or Henry George on his birth certificate was the son of Maria Webber who partnered Frederick Pudvine. It also seems that although George took the name Pudvine he knew that Frederick was not his father but possibly never knew who his real father was. Further searches on the 1881 Census brought me more information on Fanny, which, together with copies of everything I had regarding Maria Webber and her family, I posted to the living Pudvine solving another skeleton in both cupboards.

I searched the Internet for information on parish records in Kent and found an email address linked to Kent, where Ada Pudvine, daughter of Frederick Pudvine, had died. I e-mailed someone called Barry White, resisting the obvious references to his name, and received an e-mail back saying he had never come across the name Pudvine, Pudwine or Podevin. Then out of the blue I received another email from him, part of which is reproduced below:

> A few weeks ago you asked about a person called Podevin who had died in Thanet, and in my reply I said I hadn't encountered the surname in the Thanet area. No longer true – I have just seen the following baptisms in the register of St John the Baptist (Margate):
>
> 25 March 1781, William PODEVIN, son of Victor and Mary, born 2 March 1781
>
> 14 July 1782, John Francis PODEVIN, son of Victor and Mary, born 21 June 1782.

Obviously this William could not be my William as he is too old, but he or his brother could be the father of my William. I wrote back and thanked Barry and received further information part of which is reproduced below:

> To see microfilm or microfiche copies of the original registers, you will need to visit either the Canterbury Cathedral Archives (CCA) in Canterbury; or the Centre for Kentish Studies (CKS) in Maidstone; or the Society of Genealogists (SoG) in London. For the CCA and CKS you will need to obtain a pass, for the SoG you will have to pay a fee unless you are a member. If you have access to a microfiche reader, you may prefer to purchase the microfiche from the Kent FHS. For the CCA and CKS they may have copying services – if you get stuck I can dig out addresses and telephone numbers.

How kind of Barry to do this for me. A further search on the FamilySearch site brought me the following Podevins, among others, that could be related:

◆ Victor Podevin and Mary Pope, married 26th September 1774, Saint Mary the Virgin, Dover.

◆ **Their Children:**

Mary Ann	christened 1 January 1775, Saint Mary the Virgin, Dover
Victor William	christened 10 March 1776, Saint Mary the Virgin, Dover
Jenny	christened 18 May 1777, Saint Mary the Virgin, Dover
Joseph	christened 28 March 1779, Saint Mary the Virgin, Dover
William	**christened 25 March 1781, St John the Baptist, Margate**
John Francis	**christened 14 July 1782, St John the Baptist, Margate**
Martha	christened 12 March 1784, Saint Mary the Virgin, Dover
Sarah	christened 23 October 1785, Saint Mary the Virgin, Dover

As you can see the John and William that Barry White found fit perfectly with the other children of Victor and Mary.

I also received another e-mail from GenForum replying to an earlier request for information on the name Podevin that gave me similar information to the above.

I e-mailed Canterbury Cathedral asking if they could carry out research on my behalf, as I needed to weigh up the cost of travelling to Kent and the time involved if I did this research myself. I received an e-mail back from a Peter Ewart who quoted a reasonable price asking me to fill in a form he was sending me and provide as much information as I could.

September 2002

I received a postcard from Peter Ewart telling me he had received all the information I sent regarding finding William Podevin and would be in touch in due course.

So far I have established a huge amount of family history and to keep things clear I have included at the end of the book (see pages 181-186) a variety of trees listing some of the oldest confirmed ancestors downwards to Lilian Margaret Reynolds (now Hughes previously Moloney), my mother, and Brian William Marelli, my husband.

What I learned:

◆ As your research grows you should reread old information as you will spot further clues as with the Saunders family living in Albury, linking Harriet Saunders who married William.
◆ Again it proves that when having difficulty sourcing a birth, you should always consider the mother's maiden name.
◆ Following present-day leads can bring surprising results.
◆ My family research does not get any easier.
◆ My list of queries grows with each one I solve.

Family Research ONLINE

During the four years of research recorded in this book Family Research has come on leaps and bounds because of the Internet, but not everyone wants to use the Internet for researching their forbears, which is why reference to the it is limited in this book. For a full guide to researching your family history online, read my second book @ Home with Your Ancestors.com.

Epilogue

Since writing my first book I have moved on to the Internet and have uncovered more ancestors than I ever dreamt possible. I would never change those first few years because, although time consuming, it was one of the most remarkable journeys I have ever taken. But, thanks to the Internet I can now achieve what took me months in a few hours.

Family research has now become a way of life for me and is no longer a hobby but a career. You can visit my website www.dianemarelli.co.uk for more information and contact me via the site.

Good luck with your research and don't give up, you'll get there eventually.

Tips worth remembering

- Births can be and are registered late, so if you don't find what you are looking for in the correct date then always consider this possibility.
- At some point incorrect certificates will be ordered. This a risk worth taking if only to eliminate those nagging doubts or non-family members of the same name.
- It is worth doing blanket searches or one-name searches if you have a less common surname such as Marelli.
- Marriage certificates do sometimes mention other family members as witnesses. This can inform you if another ancestor is still living, married or unmarried at that time. Additionally, even if not related, a witness can still provide other clues such as why an ancestor moved to a particular area, such as William Podevin who moved from Newington in London to Albury in Surrey.
- Always check all variations of surnames when you cannot find someone where they should be. It is advisable to make a list of possible spellings the night before embarking on your research.
- If frequenting the FRC take home a bundle of birth, marriage and death forms and fill in address details and basic information to save time on your next visit.
- It is important to check changes to boundaries when looking for an ancestor in a particular area.
- Sometimes you may have to order several incorrect certificates for the same ancestor when you have no other clues. Maybe you will have to move your research sideways and look for possible siblings or come forward again to find details of descendants that might also furnish you with a fresh pointer in the right direction.
- If you cannot find a record of a certificate it is worth considering secondary names such as Stone, as with Frederick T Stone Chappell, which gave me a possible birth for him under the surname of Stone. Remember ancestors were often adopted, fostered or brought up by relatives and chose to change their names later in life.
- An ancestor can marry twice or marry two related people of the same surname as with Andrew Lugg who married sisters-in-law.

- If unable to source a birth certificate for an ancestor always consider looking under the maiden name of the mother.
- Ordering certificates from districts other than the area you believe your ancestor lived is sometimes worth the risk as with some of Frederick Pudvine's children.
- If you find an ancestor on a Census return look around the immediate locality as there could be other family members living close by.
- Searching the Census can produce information about older generations that often lived with their children.
- Always consider origins of strangely spelt surnames as you may have foreign ancestry.
- The Census can provide links in your research that you could never hope to find on certificates alone, such as the Homer Street information where I found Martino's second wife Amy living as a child, the same address that one year Martino and his first wife would live.
- The Census gives ages and places of birth of other family members.
- The Census gives more insight into the lives of your ancestors, listing neighbours and their occupations, and also building a picture of the district they lived in and whether they lodged with others or were prosperous enough to rent their own property.
- The Census gives valuable information on who is living or deceased at the time the Census is taken.
- Having the Census on CD-Rom means more search time without constraints!
- You will constantly revisit the Census as more evidence comes to light.
- Keep going back over the documents you acquire in your research – what means nothing today could provide a clue tomorrow.
- Contrary to the lack of modern-day transport our ancestors were able to and did travel extensively so do not be surprised if you find them where you least expect it.
- Information available via the Internet is amazing but should not be relied on completely and could be misleading if you do not verify finds with further evidence.
- There are monthly magazines providing you not only with interesting information about family history generally but with other sources of research or guides and much more.
- Sometimes our ancestors changed their Christian names later in life, much as people do today.

- It is possible that our ancestors were not sure of their age or date of birth or lied about their age for some reason.
- Occupations can have different titles such as painter and builder but mean the same thing.
- Old family address books can prove useful as can photographs with names or dates on the back, postcards, birthday cards, etc.
- Trawling the Internet constantly looking for family history sites, area information, churches, people, etc. is a worthwhile exercise.
- Sometimes taking a break from your research is a good idea.
- Family history is an expensive hobby but if you want results you have to be prepared to spend.
- Certificates will help you locate your ancestors on Census returns. Equally the Census will help you find certificates.
- It is worth using message board websites such as Genforum as there is always someone willing to help you.
- Never take family information for granted; stories might become muddled or exaggerated over time but they usually have an element of truth in them and were started for a reason.
- When you have a strong gut feeling about something can you really afford to ignore it?
- If you come to a dead end in your research do not give up. Try another branch of the family for a while and give your mind time to compute other potential paths to take. Never worry about asking for help.
- All family history is interesting, no matter how humble.
- You will find amazing coincidences when researching your family such as I did when I moved from one end of the country to the other only to discover I was walking in the footsteps of my ancestors.
- Sometimes you have to search a source several times before you find something e.g., the Census or the FamilySearch site.
- Some purchases of Census or Christening records on CD-Rom will not prove beneficial until further along in your research.
- Old newspapers are a valuable source to family historians.
- Be prepared to uncover distressing information.
- There are misprints and errors on most sources of information.
- An ancestor's given age can vary greatly on different sources such as birth, marriage, death, christening or Census records but it does not mean you have the wrong ancestor.
- You can never ask your family too many questions about your ancestors.
- Blanket searches for unusual family names are worth the time and effort.

- Visiting other establishments such as the Surrey History Centre can prove extremely beneficial, in my case especially when I think of the newspaper archive I found.
- Without a specific address for an ancestor searching the Census can be a laborious task but is not as expensive as randomly ordering incorrect certificates.
- Always check out various addresses you come across on the Census.
- It is worth contacting strangers if you think that possible family links exist.

So far no famous or infamous ancestors have been found in either Brian's or my family histories but we are proud of our heritage, no matter how humble, and marvel at their courage and determination to survive through difficult times. How easy our lives seem in comparison. To think this all started in memory of Bert and now Brian gifts his sons, Ian and Jason, what will hopefully become one day a comprehensive history of his family. As for me I also thank Bert because I too have been able to gift my Mother a history she never thought possible and I too have provided my many nieces and nephews with what I hope one day will also be a comprehensive family history.

Family Trees

Direct Descendants of William Podevin

Direct Descendants of John Cufley

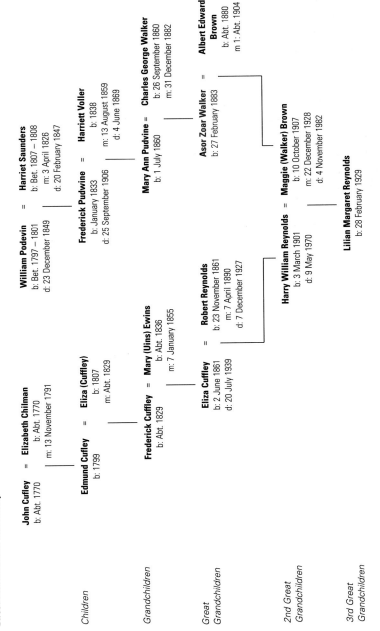

Children

Grandchildren

Great Grandchildren

2nd Great Grandchildren

3rd Great Grandchildren

John Cufley = **Elizabeth Chilman**
b: Abt. 1770   b: Abt. 1770
m: 13 November 1791

Edmund Cufley = **Eliza (Cuffley)**
b: 1799   b: 1807
m: Abt. 1829

Frederick Cuffley = **Mary (Uins) Ewins**
b: Abt. 1829   b: Abt. 1836
m: 7 January 1855

Eliza Cuffley = **Robert Reynolds**
b: 2 June 1861   b: 23 November 1861
d: 20 July 1939   m: 7 April 1890
d: 7 December 1927

William Podevin = **Harriet Saunders**
b: Bet. 1797 – 1801   b: Bet. 1807 – 1808
d: 23 December 1849   m: 3 April 1826
d: 20 February 1847

Frederick Pudvine = **Harriett Voller**
b: January 1833   b: 1838
d: 25 September 1906   m: 13 August 1859
d: 4 June 1869

Mary Ann Pudvine = **Charles George Walker**
b: 1 July 1860   b: 26 September 1860
m: 31 December 1882

Asor Zoar Walker = **Albert Edward Brown**
b: 27 February 1883   b: Abt. 1880
m 1: Abt. 1904

Harry William Reynolds = **Maggie (Walker) Brown**
b: 3 March 1901   b: 10 October 1907
d: 9 May 1970   m: 22 December 1928
d: 4 November 1982

Lilian Margaret Reynolds
b: 28 February 1929

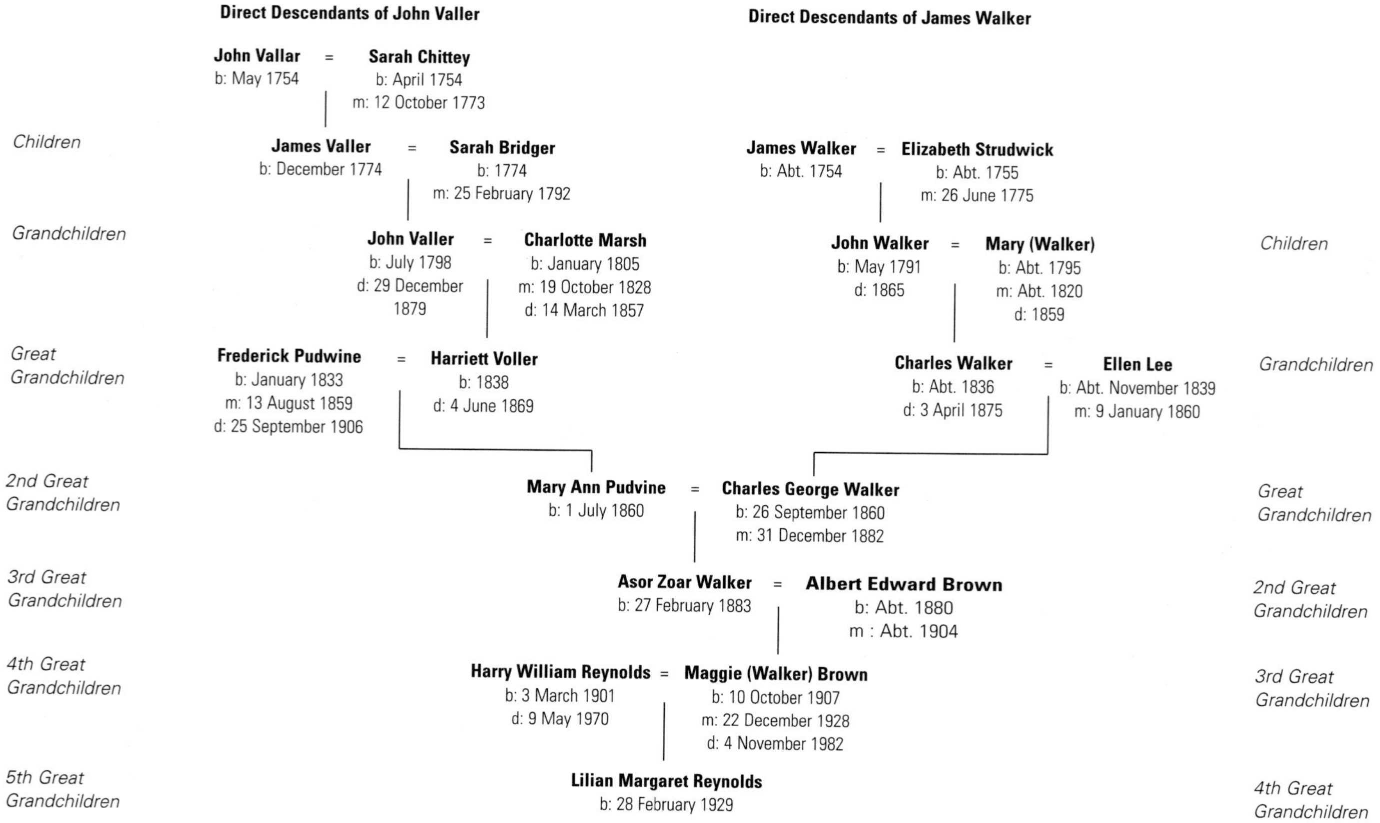

Direct Descendants of John Valler

Direct Descendants of James Walker

Children

John Vallar = **Sarah Chittey**
b: May 1754   b: April 1754
m: 12 October 1773

James Walker = **Elizabeth Strudwick**
b: Abt. 1754   b: Abt. 1755
m: 26 June 1775

Grandchildren

James Valler = **Sarah Bridger**
b: December 1774   b: 1774
m: 25 February 1792

John Walker = **Mary (Walker)**
b: May 1791   b: Abt. 1795
d: 1865   m: Abt. 1820
d: 1859

John Valler = **Charlotte Marsh**
b: July 1798   b: January 1805
d: 29 December 1879   m: 19 October 1828
d: 14 March 1857

Charles Walker = **Ellen Lee**
b: Abt. 1836   b: Abt. November 1839
d: 3 April 1875   m: 9 January 1860

Great Grandchildren

Frederick Pudwine = **Harriett Voller**
b: January 1833   b: 1838
m: 13 August 1859   d: 4 June 1869
d: 25 September 1906

Charles George Walker
b: 26 September 1860
m: 31 December 1882

2nd Great Grandchildren

Mary Ann Pudvine =
b: 1 July 1860

Asor Zoar Walker = **Albert Edward Brown**
b: 27 February 1883   b: Abt. 1880
m : Abt. 1904

3rd Great Grandchildren

Harry William Reynolds = **Maggie (Walker) Brown**
b: 3 March 1901   b: 10 October 1907
d: 9 May 1970   m: 22 December 1928
d: 4 November 1982

4th Great Grandchildren

Lilian Margaret Reynolds
b: 28 February 1929

5th Great Grandchildren

Left-side generation labels:
Children
Grandchildren
Great Grandchildren
2nd Great Grandchildren
3rd Great Grandchildren
4th Great Grandchildren
5th Great Grandchildren

Direct Descendants of John Lee

John Lee = **Jane Cobbett** ??
b: Abt. 1815   m: 4 February 1837

Charles Walker = **Ellen Lee**   *Children*
b: Abt. 1836   b: Abt. November 1839
d: 3 April 1875   m: 9 January 1860

Mary Ann Pudvine = **Charles George Walker**   *Grandchildren*
b: 1 July 1860   b: 26 September 1860
m: 31 December 1882

Asor Zoar Walker = **Albert Edward Brown**   *Great*
b: 27 February 1883   b: Abt. 1880   *Grandchildren*
m : Abt. 1904

Harry William Reynolds = **Maggie (Walker) Brown**   *2nd Great*
b: 3 March 1901   b: 10 October 1907   *Grandchildren*
d: 9 May 1970   m: 22 December 1928
d: 4 November 1982

Lilian Margaret Reynolds   *3rd Great*
b: 28 February 1929   *Grandchildren*

Direct Descendants of John Charitie Plummer

John Charitie Plummer = **Hannah Comfort**
b: Abt. 1825

Children   **William Plummer** = **Susan Jordan**
b: 1 January 1845   b: Abt. 1841
m: 19 November 1865

Grandchildren   **Martino Marelli**   **Amy (Alice) Plummer**
b: 20 January 1852 =   b: Abt. 1867
d: 14 February 1940   m: 25 December 1891
d: 11 November 1912

Great   **Albert Marelli**   **Lillian Lucretia**
Grandchildren   b: 25 December 1892 =   **Chappell**
d: 13 July 1974   b: 10 April 1892
m: 25 July 1912
d: 18 December 1970

2nd Great   **Albert (Bert) Marelli** = **Dorothy Ethel Olive Lord**
Grandchildren   b: 20 November 1915   b: 9 July 1923
d: 18 June 1998   m: 17 April 1943
d: 17 May 1964

3rd Great   **Brian Marelli**
Grandchildren   b: 9 October 1943

Direct Descendants of Broughton Reynolds

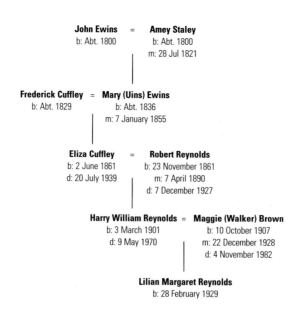

Broughton Reynolds = **Jane Arabella Wilson**
b: Abt. 1838   b: Abt. 1840

Children

Robert Reynolds = **Eliza Cuffley**
b: 23 November 1861   b: 2 June 1861
d: 7 December 1927   m: 7 April 1890
d: 20 July 1939

Grandchildren

Harry William Reynolds = **Maggie (Walker) Brown**
b: 3 March 1901   b: 10 October 1907
d: 9 May 1970   m: 22 December 1928
d: 4 November 1982

Great
Grandchildren

Lilian Margaret Reynolds
b: 28 February 1929

Direct Descendants of John Ewins

John Ewins = **Amey Staley**
b: Abt. 1800   b: Abt. 1800
m: 28 Jul 1821

Frederick Cuffley = **Mary (Uins) Ewins**
b: Abt. 1829   b: Abt. 1836
m: 7 January 1855

Eliza Cuffley = **Robert Reynolds**
b: 2 June 1861   b: 23 November 1861
d: 20 July 1939   m: 7 April 1890
d: 7 December 1927

Harry William Reynolds = **Maggie (Walker) Brown**
b: 3 March 1901   b: 10 October 1907
d: 9 May 1970   m: 22 December 1928
d: 4 November 1982

Lilian Margaret Reynolds
b: 28 February 1929

Direct Descendants of Martino Marelli

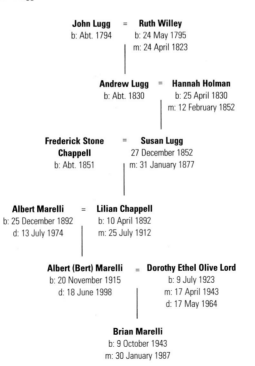

Martino Marelli	**Amy (Alice) Plummer**	
b: 20 January 1852 =	b: Abt. 1867	
d: 14 February 1940	m: 25 December 1891	
	d: 11 November 1912	

Albert Marelli
b: 25 December 1892 =
d: 13 July 1974

Lillian Lucretia
Chappell
b: 10 April 1892
m: 25 July 1912
d: 18 December 1970

Albert (Bert) Marelli = **Dorothy Ethel Olive Lord**
b: 20 November 1915   b: 9 July 1923
d: 18 June 1998   m: 17 April 1943
                            d: 17 May 1964

Brian Marelli
b: 9 October 1943

Direct Descendants of John Lugg

John Lugg = **Ruth Willey**
b: Abt. 1794   b: 24 May 1795
                 m: 24 April 1823

Andrew Lugg = **Hannah Holman**
b: Abt. 1830   b: 25 April 1830
                   m: 12 February 1852

Frederick Stone = **Susan Lugg**
Chappell   27 December 1852
b: Abt. 1851   m: 31 January 1877

Albert Marelli = **Lilian Chappell**
b: 25 December 1892   b: 10 April 1892
d: 13 July 1974   m: 25 July 1912

Albert (Bert) Marelli = **Dorothy Ethel Olive Lord**
b: 20 November 1915   b: 9 July 1923
d: 18 June 1998   m: 17 April 1943
                           d: 17 May 1964

Brian Marelli
b: 9 October 1943
m: 30 January 1987

Direct Descendants of James Holman

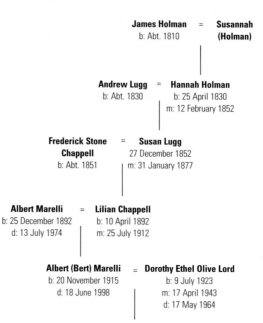

James Holman = Susannah
b: Abt. 1810   (Holman)

Andrew Lugg = Hannah Holman
b: Abt. 1830   b: 25 April 1830
m: 12 February 1852

Frederick Stone = Susan Lugg
Chappell   27 December 1852
b: Abt. 1851   m: 31 January 1877

Albert Marelli = Lilian Chappell
b: 25 December 1892   b: 10 April 1892
d: 13 July 1974   m: 25 July 1912

Albert (Bert) Marelli = Dorothy Ethel Olive Lord
b: 20 November 1915   b: 9 July 1923
d: 18 June 1998   m: 17 April 1943
                        d: 17 May 1964

Brian Marelli
b: 9 October 1943
m: 30 January 1987

Outline of the life of Martino Marelli 1852 – 1940

Martino was born on 20 January 1852 in the Provincial Foundlings Home, Milan. Between the ages of approximately 18 and 23 years Martino arrived in London, England and up until the present day his first known address in London is Nelson Street, Holborn. Between arriving in England *c.*1872 and marrying his first wife Ellen he at least had learnt to write his name in English, as he was able to sign his name on his marriage certificate. He was married on 1 February 1875 to Ellen McDonald, daughter of a Tailor, who was also living in Holborn.

Martino and Ellen's first daughter, also called Ellen, was born on 7 May 1876 in Holborn 'Lying In' Hospital. They were lodging in Macclesfield Street north of City Road, Holborn. At this time Martino was working as a carman and now aged 24 years. Martino must have been reasonably employed because 'Lying In' hospitals were intended for the 'wives of poor industrious tradesmen'.

By 1877 Martino had moved his family to new lodgings in Sudely Street, Islington where his second daughter Rosa was born on 27 August 1877. Martino still held his job of carman. Rosa would die 10 weeks later of bronchitis.

Within the year Martino and Ellen and their eldest daughter Ellen, aged two years, were living at different lodgings in Lambeth. Martino was still working as a carman when his son Martin was born on 29 August 1878.

Between 1878 and 1880 Martino had moved his family to Oakley Street in Lambeth and had changed his occupation to ice merchant when on 23 June 1880 another daughter Ada is born. It is believed his new occupation of ice merchant must have been his own business or he would have been called an ice seller. Within three months of Martin's birth Martino had moved his family once again to Tyers Street, Lambeth, a home he and family shared with a gentleman called Henry Lorenz, a fishmonger (verified by 1881 Census). As Martino's family grew and he began to prosper it is assumed he moved constantly to provide better lodgings for his family because by the time his daughter Matilda was born in October 1882 the family had moved once more to Homer Street, Lambeth. On Matilda's birth certificate it states Martino's occupation is carman again but Ellen his wife registered Matilda's birth so this could be an error because by the time Rosalier, his fifth daughter, was born in 1884 his occupation is again ice merchant. Martino and his family of four children were now living in 8 Lower Marsh, Lambeth.

Martino and family settled in Lower Marsh but tragedy would strike again in 1886 with the birth and death of Martino's daughter, Amelia, who was found dead in bed aged only three months. The heartbreak did not end there, as little Rosalier now aged 3, died in 1888 and in that same year Martino would lose his wife Ellen who was just 30 years of age. Martino had now endured the loss of three children and his young wife.

A widower with a young family of four children, Martino was alone and would have to seek help caring for his children in order for him to continue providing for them. This is only supposition but it is believed that Martino had made the acquaintance of a gentleman by the name of William Plummer some years previously. Both William and Martino had lived at the same address of Homer Street, Lambeth within one year of each other. (This is verified by the 1881 Census.) In 1888 William Plummer's daughter called Amy was 21 years of age and it is possible that Martino employed her as a child-minder because by Christmas Day 1891 Martino and Amy were husband and wife, with the sanction of Amy's parents who were witnesses at their wedding. On Christmas Day, one year to the day after his marriage to Amy, their first child Albert was born in 1892.

Martino had now expanded his business from dealing in ice and had also become a fishmonger. Martino and Amy stayed at Lower Marsh where it is believed they lived above Martino's thriving business as he now had two shop assistants, of Italian origin lodging with him (verified by the 1891 Census). In August 1894 Martino and Amy's second child Amelia was born (named presumably after the daughter Martino has lost during his first marriage to Ellen). William's birth followed Amelia's in April

1896 but by now Martino had purchased a house in Long Beach Road, Battersea. There is a little confusion here because on 17 May 1897 Martino was naturalised as a British subject but his address is given as 138 Lower Marsh. (We know that Martino expanded his business at some stage into a small chain of fish and chip shops. Perhaps this was another business address because by 1897 he was definitely living in Long Beach Road where he would live out the rest of his life.)

Presumably Long Beach is a large house because by 1898 another daughter, by the name of Amy, would be born. Martino now had eight children living with him ranging in ages from 22 years down. Life was looking good for Martino. His eldest son Martin had followed in his father's footsteps and worked in the family business and in December 1899 another daughter Kathleen was born. Sadly Martino's happiness would be short-lived as Martin died at the age of 22 in March 1901. Martino was now 49 years of age. Three more children would be born following Martin's death: Winifred in March 1902, Henry in 1903 and Philomena in 1906. Martino had sired 15 children during the term of his two marriages.

In between the last three births the marriage of Ada, Martino's daughter from his first marriage, would occur in 1902 and that of Matilda, another daughter of the same marriage, in 1908. The first child, Albert, from Martino's second marriage to Amy, would marry in July 1912 but Martino would lose his second wife later that same year, when she was 45 years of age.

Martino was now 60 years old and had suffered the death of two wives and four children from his first marriage. Little is known about the next few years but it is believed William or Henry, or both, worked in the family business while Albert went his own way. In 1921 Martino would see his daughter Amy married but would suffer the death of his second daughter called Amelia, from his second marriage to Amy in 1922.

Of the remaining children it is known that William married in 1924, Kathleen in 1925 and Philomena in 1926. Not all marriages have been sourced at this point in time.

Martino Marelli lived until he was 88 years of age and would die on 13 February 1940. He was buried in Brookwood Cemetery with his son Martin who had died nearly 40 years previously.

Useful research sources

Websites

1837online: www.1837online.com/ – now known as www.findmypast.com
Alan Godfrey Maps: www.alangodfreymaps.co.uk/
Ancestors Magazine & The National Archive:
    www.nationalarchives.gov.uk/shop/ancestors.htm
Ancestors Magazine: www.ancestorsmagazine.co.uk/
Ancestry.co.uk: www.ancestry.co.uk/
Author: www.dianemarelli.co.uk
Cemsearch UK: www.cemsearch.co.uk/
Chappell Family Tree Site & Others: www.stevenjones.me.uk/
Cyndi's List: www.cyndislist.com/
Family Historian Software: www.family-historian.co.uk/
Family History Monthly: www.familyhistorymonthly.com/
Family Tree Magazine & Practical Family History:
    www.family-tree.co.uk/
Family Tree Maker Software: www.familytreemaker.com
Free BMD: www.freebmd.org.uk
Genealogy Quest: www.genealogy-quest.com/glossaries/diseases1.html
General Register Office: www.gro.gov.uk
Genes Reunited www.genesreunited.co.uk/
Genuki British Isles Genealogy; Genuki Contents &
    Site Map: www.genuki.org.uk/contents/
Historical Directories: www.historicaldirectories.org/hd/index.asp
Legacy Family Tree Software: www.legacyfamilytree.com/
Map Quest: www.mapquest.co.uk/
My History Software: www.my-history.co.uk/
Old Maps: www.old-maps.co.uk/
Peter Christian Internet Guides to Family History: www.spub.co.uk/
Registration Districts in England and Wales (1837-1974) Genuki:
    www.fhsc.org.uk/genuki/reg/
Scottish Graveyards & UK Links:
    www.scottishgraveyards.org.uk/
The British Library Online: www.uk.olivesoftware.com
The Canal Museum: www.canalmuseum.org.uk/ice/index.html
The Church of Jesus Christ of Latter Day Saints: www.familysearch.org

The Commonwealth War Graves Commission: www.cwgc.org/
The Federation of Family History www.ffhs.org.uk/
The Hall Genealogy: www.rmhh.co.uk/
The National Archive: www.nationalarchives.gov.uk/
The Old Bailey: www.oldbaileyonline.org/
The Society of Genealogy: www.sog.org.uk/
The Surrey History Centre: www.surreycc.gov.uk/
The Victorian Dictionary: /www.victorianlondon.org/
UK & Ireland – Genuki Home Page: www.genuki.org.uk/
Your Family Tree Magazine: www.yourfamilytreemag.co.uk/

Family History & Genealogical Societies

IRELAND

Genealogical Soc of Ireland
CONTACT: Mr Michael Merrigan, Hon. Secretary, 11 Desmond
Avenue, Dun Laoghaire, Co. Dublin, Ireland
e: GenSocIreland@iol.ie
w: http://welcome.to/GenealogyIreland

Irish FHS
CONTACT: c/o The Secretary, PO Box 36, Naas, Co Kildare, Ireland
e: ifhs@eircom.net
w: http://welcome.to/GenealogyIreland

Irish Genealogical Research Society
CONTACT: Peter Manning, 18 Stratford Avenue, Rainham, Gillingham,
Kent, ME8 0EP
e: info@igrsoc.org
w: www.igrsoc.org

North of Ireland FHS
CONTACT: G M Siberry, c/o Graduate School of Education, The
Queen's University of Belfast, 69 University Street, Belfast, NI BT7 1HL
e: enquiries@nifhs.org
w: www.nifhs.org

ENGLAND

BEDFORDSHIRE
Bedfordshire FHS
CONTACT: Mrs Anne Simmonds, PO Box 214, Bedford MK42 9RX
e: bfhs@bfhs.org.uk
w: www.bfhs.org.uk

BERKSHIRE
Berkshire FHS
CONTACT: The Secretary, Berkshire FHS, Yeomanry House,
131 Castle Hill, Reading, RG1 7TJ
e: secretary@berksfhs.org.uk
w: www.berksfhs.org.uk

BUCKINGHAMSHIRE
Buckinghamshire FHS
CONTACT: The Secretary, c/o PO Box 403, Aylesbury,
Buckinghamshire HP21 7GU
e: society@bucksfhs.org.uk
w: www.bucksfhs.org.uk

CAMBRIDGESHIRE
Cambridgeshire FHS
CONTACT: David Wratten, 43 Eachard Road, Cambridge CB3 0HZ
e: secretary@cfhs.org.uk
w: www.cfhs.org.uk

Cambridge University H&GS
CONTACT: c/o Crossfield House, Dale Road, Stanton, Bury St Edmunds,
Suffolk IP31 2DY
e: mlm39@hermes.cam.ac.uk
w: www.cam.ac.uk/societies/cuhags

Fenland FHS
CONTACT: Judy Green, Rose Hall, Walpole Bank, Walpole St.Andrew,
Wisbech PE14 7JD
e: judy.green@farming.me.uk
w: www.fenlandfhs.org.uk

CHANNEL ISLANDS
Channel Islands FHS
CONTACT: Mrs P A Neale, Secretary, PO Box 507, St Helier, Jersey
JE4 5TN
w: user.itl.net/~glen/AbouttheChannelIslandsFHS.html

La Société Guernesiaise (FH Section)
CONTACT: The Secretary, Family History Section of La Société
Guernesiaise, PO Box 314, Candie, St Peter Port, Guernsey GY1 3TG
w: www.societe.org.gg/sections/familyhistorysec.htm

CHESHIRE
The FHS of Cheshire
CONTACT: Mike Craig, 10 Dunns Lane, Ashton, Chester CH3 8BU
e: info@fhsc.org.uk
w: www.fhsc.org.uk

North Cheshire FHS
CONTACT: Mrs Rhoda Clarke, 2 Denham Drive, Bramhall, Stockport,
Cheshire SK7 2AT
e: r.demercado@ntlworld.com
w: www.ncfhs.org.uk

CORNWALL
Cornwall FHS
CONTACT: The Administrator, 5 Victoria Square, Truro, Cornwall TR1 2RS
e: secretary@cornwallfhs.com
w: www.cornwallfhs.com

CUMBERLAND
Cumbria FHS
CONTACT: Mrs S Dench, 279 Newtown Road, Carlisle, Cumbria CA2 7LS
w: www.cumbriafhs.com

Furness FHS
CONTACT: Miss J Fairbairn, 64 Cowlarns Road, Barrow-in-Furness,
Cumbria LA14 4HJ
e: julia.fairbairn@virgin.net
w: www.furnessfhs.co.uk

DERBYSHIRE
Derbyshire FHS
CONTACT: Mr Dave Bull, Bridge Chapel House, St Mary's Bridge,
Sowter Rd, Derby DE1 3AT
w: www.dfhs.org.uk

Chesterfield & District FHS
CONTACT: D Rogers, Correspondence Secretary, 2 Highlow Close,
Loundsley Green,Chesterfield, Derbyshire S40 4PG
e: mail@cadfhs.org.uk
w: www.cadfhs.org.uk

DEVON
Devon FHS
CONTACT: The Secretary, Devon FHS, PO Box 9, Exeter, Devon EX2 6YP
e: secretary@devonfhs.org.uk
w: www.devonfhs.org.uk

DORSET
Dorset FHS
CONTACT: Dorset FHS, Treetops Research Centre, Suite 5 Stanley House,
3 Fleets Lane, Poole, Dorset, BH15 3AJ
e: contact@dorsetfhs.org.uk
w: www.dorsetfhs.org.uk

Somerset & Dorset FHS
CONTACT: The Secretary, PO Box 4502, Sherborne DT9 6YL
e: society@sdfhs.org
w: www.sdfhs.org

DURHAM
Northumberland & Durham FHS
CONTACT: Mrs Frances Norman, 23 Monkton Avenue, Simonside,
South Shields, Tyne & Wear NE34 9RX
e: frances@fnorman.fsnet.co.uk
w: www.ndfhs.org.uk

Cleveland, N. Yorkshire & S. Durham FHS
CONTACT: Mr A. Sampson, 1 Oxgang Close, Redcar,
Cleveland TS10 4ND
w: www.clevelandfhs.org.uk/

ESSEX
Essex SFH
CONTACT: Mrs A Church, Windyridge, 32 Parsons Heath, Colchester, Essex CO4 3HX
e: secretary@esfh.org.uk
w: www.esfh.org.uk

East of London FHS
CONTACT: Ian Whaley, 46 Brights Avenue, Rainham, Essex RM13 9NW
e: eolfhs@btopenworld.com
w: www.eolfhs.org.uk

Waltham Forest FHS
CONTACT: Mr B.F. Burton, 49 Sky Peals Rd, Woodford Green, Essex IG8 9NE

GLOUCESTERSHIRE
Bristol & Avon FHS
CONTACT: Margaret Smith, 7 Henleaze Park Drive, Bristol, BS9 4LH
e: secretary@bafhs.org.uk
w: www.bafhs.org.uk

Gloucestershire FHS
CONTACT: Alex Wood, 37 Barrington Drive, Hucclecote, Gloucestershire GL3 3BT
e: gfhs@blueyonder.co.uk
w: www.gfhs.org.uk

HAMPSHIRE
Hampshire Genealogical Society
CONTACT: Mrs. Sheila Brine, 3 Elaine Gardens, Lovedean, Waterlooville, Hants PO8 9QS
e: secretary@hgs-online.org.uk
w: www.hgs-online.org.uk

Isle of Wight FHS
CONTACT: Mrs Brenda Dodgson, 9 Forest Dell, Winford, Sandown, I.O.W. P036 0LG
e: brendave@dodgson9.freeserve.co.uk
w: www.isle-of-wight-fhs.co.uk

HEREFORDSHIRE
Herefordshire FHS
CONTACT: Brian Prosser, 6 Birch Meadow, Gosmore Road, Clehonger,
Hereford, HR2 9RH
e: prosser_brian@hotmail.com
w: www.rootsw.com/~ukhfhs/

HERTFORDSHIRE
Hertfordshire FHS
CONTACT: Mrs Amelia Cheek, 38 Roselands Avenue, Hoddesdon,
Herts EN11 9BB
e: secretary@hertsfhs.org.uk
w: www.hertsfhs.org.uk

Letchworth & District FH Group
CONTACT: Mrs Helen Fitzgibbons, 2 Cross Street,
Letchworth Garden City, Herts SG6 4UD
e: hfitz45@ntlworld.com
w: www.letchworthgardencity.net/LDFHG/Index.html

Royston & District FHS
CONTACT: Mrs Kay Curtis, "Baltana" London Road, Barkway,
 Nr Royston, Herts SG8 8EY
e: kay.tails@virgin.net
w: www.roystonfhs.org

HUNTINGDONSHIRE
Huntingdon FHS
CONTACT: Mrs C. Kesseler, 42 Crowhill, Godmanchester,
Huntingdon, Cambs PE29 2NR
e: secretary@huntsfhs.org.uk
w: www.huntsfhs.org.uk

ISLE OF MAN
Isle of Man FHS
CONTACT: Mrs Priscilla Lewthwaite, Pear Tree Cottage,
Lhergy Cripperty, Union Mills, Isle of Man IM4 4NF

ISLE OF WIGHT
Isle of Wight FHS
CONTACT: Mrs Brenda Dodgson, 9 Forest Dell, Winford, Sandown,
I.O.W, P036 0LG
e: brendave@dodgson9.freeserve.co.uk
w: www.isle-of-wight-fhs.co.uk

KENT
Kent FHS
CONTACT: Mrs Kristin Slater, Bullockstone Farm, Bullockstone Road,
Herne, Kent CT6 7NL
e: kristn@globalnet.co.uk
w: www.kfhs.org.uk

Folkestone & District FHS
CONTACT: Mrs Janet Powell, Kingsmill Down, Hastingleigh, Ashford,
Kent TN25 5JJ
e: secretary@folkfhs.org.uk
w: www.folkfhs.org.uk

North West Kent FHS
CONTACT: Mrs Vera Bailey, 58 Clarendon Gardens, Stone, Dartford,
Kent DA2 6EZ
e: secretary@nwkfhs.org.uk
w: www.nwkfhs.org.uk

Tunbridge Wells FHS
CONTACT: Roy Thompson, 5 College Drive, Tunbridge Wells, Kent
TN2 3PN
e: roythompson@mailsnare.net
w: www.tunwells-fhs.co.uk

Woolwich & District FHS
CONTACT: Mrs Edna Reynolds, 54 Parkhill Road, Bexley, Kent DA5 1HY
e: FrEdnaFHS@aol.com

LANCASHIRE
Cumbria Family History Society
Ulpha, 32 Granadas Road, Denton, Manchester M34 2LJ

General Register Office
Certificate Services Section, PO Box 2, Southport, PR8 2JD
T: 0845 603 7788

Lancashire FH & Heraldry Soc
CONTACT: Joyce Monks, 21 Baytree Road, Clayton le Woods PR6 7JW
e: secretary@lfhhs.org.uk
w: www.lfhhs.org.uk

Manchester & Lancashire FHS
CONTACT: Judith Sellers, c/o M&LFHS, Clayton House, 59 Piccadilly,
Manchester M1 2AQ
e: office@mlfhs.org.uk
w: www.mlfhs.org.uk

Furness FHS
CONTACT: Miss J Fairbairn, 64 Cowlarns Road, Barrow-in-Furness,
Cumbria LA14 4HJ
e: julia.fairbairn@virgin.net
w: www.furnessfhs.co.uk

Lancashire Parish Register Society
CONTACT: Alan Kenwright, 19 Churton Grove, Shevington Moor,
Wigan, Lancs WN6 0SZ
e: akenwright@yahoo.com
w: www.lprs.org.uk

Lancaster FH Group
CONTACT: Mrs P.Harrison, 116 Bowerham Road, Lancaster LA1 4HL
e: secretary@lfhg.org
w: www.lfhg.org

Liverpool & SW Lancs FHS
CONTACT: Mr David Guiver, 11 Bushbys Lane, Formby, Liverpool
L37 2DX
e: DavidGuiver@aol.com
w: www.liverpool-genealogy.org.uk

North Meols FHS
CONTACT: Jane Scarisbrick, 6 Millars Place, Marshside,
Southport PR9 9FU
e: jane.scarisbrick@virgin.net
w: www.nmfhssouthport.co.uk

Ormskirk & District FHS
CONTACT: ODFHS, PO Box 213 Aughton, Ormskirk, Lancs L39 5WT
e: secretary@odfhs.org.uk
w: www.odfhs.org.uk

Wigan F&LHS
CONTACT: John Wogan, 678 Warrington Road, Goose Green, Wigan,
Lancs WN3 6XN
e: johnwogan@blueyonder.co.uk
w: www.ffhs.org.uk/members/wigan.htm

LEICESTERSHIRE
Leicestershire & Rutland FHS
CONTACT: Mrs Joan Rowbottom, 37 Cyril Street, Leicester LE3 2FF
e: secretary@lrfhs.org.uk
w: www.lrfhs.org.uk

LINCOLNSHIRE
Lincolnshire FHS
CONTACT: Brenda Coulson, 57 Lupin Road, Lincoln LN2 4GB
e: secretary@lincolnshirefhs.org.uk
w: www.lincolnshirefhs.org.uk

Isle of Axholme FHS
CONTACT: Norma Neill (Secretary), 'Colywell', 43 Commonside,
Westwoodside, Doncaster DN9 2AR
e: secretary@axholme-fhs.org.uk
w: www.axholme-fhs.org.uk

LONDON / MIDDLESEX AREA
East of London FHS
CONTACT: Ian Whaley, 46 Brights Avenue, Rainham, Essex RM13 9NW
e: eolfhs@btopenworld.com
w: www.eolfhs.org.uk

East Surrey FHS
CONTACT: ESFHS, 119 Keevil Drive, London SW19 6TF
e: secretary@eastsurreyfhs.org.uk
w: www.eastsurreyfhs.org.uk

Guild of One-Name Studies
CONTACT: c/o Hon Sec, Box G, 14 Charterhouse Buildings,
Goswell Road, London EC1M 7BA
e: guild@one-name.org
w: www.one-name.org
T: 0800 011 2182

Hillingdon FHS
CONTACT: Mrs G. May, 20 Moreland Drive, Gerrards Cross, Bucks
SL9 8BB
e: Gillmay@dial.pipex.com
w: www.hfhs.co.uk

International Society for British Genealogy & Family History
Kathleen W. Hinckley, CGRS Business Manager
International Society for British Genealogy & Family History
PO Box 350459, Westminster, CO 80035-0459
e: isbgfh@yahoo.com
w: www.isbgfh.org

London Westminster & Middlesex FHS
CONTACT: Mr & Mrs Pyemont, 57 Belvedere Way, Kenton, Harrow,
Middlesex HA3 9XQ
w: www.lnmfhs.dircon.co.uk

North West Kent FHS
CONTACT: Mrs Vera Bailey, 58 Clarendon Gardens, Stone, Dartford,
Kent DA2 6EZ
e: secretary@nwkfhs.org.uk
w: www.nwkfhs.org.uk

Society of Genealogists
14 Charterhouse Buildings, Goswell Road, London EC1M 7BA
T: 0207 251 8799

Waltham Forest FHS
CONTACT: Mr B.F. Burton, 49 Sky Peals Rd, Woodford Green, Essex
IG8 9NE

West Middlesex FHS
CONTACT: Tony Simpson, 32 The Avenue Bedford Park, Chiswick,
London W4 1HT
e: secretary@west-middlesex-fhs.org.uk
w: www.west-middlesex-fhs.org.uk

Westminster & Central Middlesex FHS
Woolwich & District FHS
CONTACT: Mrs Edna Reynolds, 54 Parkhill Road, Bexley, Kent DA5 1HY

NORFOLK
Norfolk FHS
CONTACT: Mr Edmund G Perry, Kirby Hall, 70 St Giles Street,
Norwich NR2 1LS
e: nfhs@paston.co.uk
w: www.norfolkfhs.org.uk/

Mid-Norfolk FHS
CONTACT: Mrs Kate Easdown, Secretary MNFHS, 47 Greengate,
Swanton Morley, Dereham, Norfolk NR20 4LX
e: keasdown@aol.com
w: www.mnfhs.freeuk.com

NORTHAMPTONSHIRE
Northamptonshire FHS
CONTACT: Mr Keith Steggles, 22 Godwin Walk, Ryehill, Northampton
NN5 7RW
e: secretary@northants-fhs.org
w: www.northants-fhs.org

Peterborough & District FHS
CONTACT: Mrs Margaret Brewster, 111 New Road, Woodston,
Peterborough PE2 9HE
e: meandmygarden@hotmail.com
w: www.peterborofhs.org.uk

NORTHUMBERLAND
Northumberland & Durham FHS
CONTACT: Mrs Frances Norman, 23 Monkton Avenue, Simonside,
South Shields, Tyne & Wear NE34 9R
e: frances@fnorman.fsnet.co.uk
w: www.ndfhs.org.uk

NOTTINGHAMSHIRE
Nottinghamshire FHS
CONTACT: Stuart Mason, 26 Acorn Bank, West Bridgford,
Nottingham NG2 7DU
e: secretary@nottsfhs.org.uk
w: www.nottsfhs.org.uk

Mansfield & District FHS
CONTACT: Miss B.E. Flintham, 15 Cranmer Grove, Mansfield, Notts
NG19 7JR

OXFORDSHIRE
Oxfordshire FHS
CONTACT: Mrs J. Kennedy, 19 Mavor Close, Woodstock, Oxford
OX20 1YL
e: secretary@ofhs.org.uk
w: www.ofhs.org.uk

RUTLAND
Leicestershire & Rutland FHS
CONTACT: The Secretary, c/o 51 New Street, Barrow Upon Soar,
Leicestershire LE12 8PA
e: secretary@lrfhs.org.uk
w: www.lrfhs.org.uk

SHROPSHIRE
Shropshire FHS
CONTACT: Mrs D. Hills, Redhillside, Ludlow Road, Church Stretton,
Shropshire SY6 6AD
e: secretary@sfhs.org.uk
w: www.sfhs.org.uk

SOMERSET
Bristol & Avon FHS
CONTACT: Margaret Smith, 7 Henleaze Park Drive, Bristol BS9 4LH
e: secretary@bafhs.org.uk
w: www.bafhs.org.uk

Somerset & Dorset FHS
CONTACT: The Secretary, PO Box 4502, Sherborne DT9 6YL
e: society@sdfhs.org
w: www.sdfhs.org

Weston-Super-Mare FHS
CONTACT: Brian Airey, 125 Totterdown Road, Weston-Super-Mare,
BS23 4LW
e: secretary@wsmfhs.org.uk
w: www.wsmfhs.org.uk

STAFFORDSHIRE
Birmingham & Midland SGH
CONTACT: Mrs Jackie Cotterill, 5 Sanderling Court, Kidderminster
DY10 4TS
e: gensec@ bmsgh.org
w: www.bmsgh.org

Burntwood FH Group
CONTACT: Jennifer Lee, 8 Peakes Road, Rugeley, Staffs WS15 2LY
e: jennifer.lee@care4free.net
w: www.geocities.com/bfhg1986

SUFFOLK
Felixstowe FHS
CONTACT: Mrs J.S. Campbell, 7 Victoria Road, Felixstowe, Suffolk
IP11 7PT

Suffolk FHS
CONTACT: Mrs P Marshall, 2 Flash Corner, Theberton, Leiston,
Suffolk IP16 4RW
e: admin@suffolkfhs.org.uk
w: www.suffolkfhs.org.uk

SURREY
East Surrey FHS
CONTACT: ESFHS, 119 Keevil Drive, London SW19 6TF
e: secretary@eastsurreyfhs.org.uk
w: www.eastsurreyfhs.org.uk

Surrey History Centre
130 Goldsworth Road, Woking, Surrey GU21 6ND
T: 01483 518737

The National Archives
Kew, Richmond, Surrey, TW9 4DU
T: 020 8876 3444

West Surrey FHS
CONTACT: Mrs Ann Sargeant, 21 Sheppard Road, Basingstoke, Hants
RG21 3HT
e: secretary@wsfhs.org
w: www.wsfhs.org

SUSSEX
Eastbourne & District (Family Roots) FHS
CONTACT: Mr John Crane, 8 Park Lane, Hampden Park, Eastbourne
BN21 2UT
e: johnandval.crane@tiscali.co.uk
w: www.eastbournefhs.org.uk

Hastings & Rother FHS
CONTACT: Linda Smith, 355 Bexhill Road, St Leonards-on-Sea,
East Sussex TN38 8AJ
e: enquiries@hrfhs.org.uk
w: www.hrfhs.org.uk

Sussex FHG
CONTACT: Mrs Val Orr, 54 Heron Way, Horsham, Sussex RH13 6DL
e: secretary@sfhg.org.uk
w: www.sfhg.org.uk

Tunbridge Wells FHS
CONTACT: Roy Thompson, 5 College Drive, Tunbridge Wells, Kent
TN2 3PN
e: roythompson@mailsnare.net
w: www.tunwells-fhs.co.uk

WARWICKSHIRE
Birmingham & Midland SGH
CONTACT: Mrs Jackie Cotterill, 5 Sanderling Court, Kidderminster
DY10 4TS
e: gensec@ bmsgh.org
w: www.bmsgh.org

Coventry FHS
CONTACT: Angela Crabtree, Barton Fields Cottage, 1 Barton Fields,
Ecton, Nothants NN6 0BF
e: gen-sec@covfhs.org
w: www.covfhs.org

Nuneaton & North Warwickshire FHS
CONTACT: Peter Lee, PO Box 2282, Nuneaton, Warwickshire CV11 9ZT
e: Nuneatonian2000@aol.com
w: www.nnwfhs.org.uk

Rugby FHG
CONTACT: Mr John A Chard, Springfields, Rocheberie Way, Rugby
CV22 6EG
e: j.chard@ntlworld.com
w: www.rugbyfhg.co.uk

Warwickshire FHS
CONTACT: Chairman, 44 Abbotts Lane, Coventry CV1 4AZ
e: chairman@wfhs.org.uk
w: www.wfhs.org.uk

WESTMORLAND
Cumbria FHS
CONTACT: Mrs S Dench, 279 Newtown Road, Carlisle,
Cumbria CA2 7LS
w: www.cumbriafhs.com

WILTSHIRE
Wiltshire FHS
CONTACT: Mrs Diana Grout, 42 Stokehill, Hilperton, Trowbridge,
Wiltshire BA14 7TJ
e: secretary@wiltshirefhs.co.uk
w: www.wiltshirefhs.co.uk

WORCESTERSHIRE
Birmingham & Midland SGH
CONTACT: Mrs Jackie Cotterill, 5 Sanderling Court, Kidderminster
DY10 4TS
e: gensec@ bmsgh.org
w: www.bmsgh.org

Malvern FH Society
CONTACT: Betty Firth, Apartment 5, Severn Grange, Northwick Road,
Bevere, Worcester WR3 7RE
e: betty.firth@virgin.net
w: www.mfhs.org.uk

YORKSHIRE
East Yorkshire FHS
CONTACT: Mrs M. Oliver, 12 Carlton Drive, Aldbrough,
East Yorkshire HU11 4SF
e: secretary@eyfhs.org.uk
w: www.eyfhs.org.uk

London Group of Yorkshire FHSs
CONTACT: Ian Taylor, 1 Waverley Way, Carshalton Beeches, Surrey
SM5 3LQ
e: ian-taylor@blueyonder.co.uk
w: www.genuki.org.uk/big/eng/YKS/Misc/FHS/

Yorkshire Archaeological Society FH Section
CONTACT: Mrs J Butler, Secretary, c/o YAS, Claremont,
23 Clarendon Road, Leeds LS2 9NZ
e: secretary@yorkshireroots.org.uk
w: www.yorkshireroots.org.uk

YORKSHIRE – EAST RIDING

City of York & District FHS
CONTACT: Mrs Mary Varley, Ascot House, Cherry Tree Avenue,
Newton-on-Ouse, York YO30 2BN
e: secretary@yorkfamilyhistory.org.uk
w: www.yorkfamilyhistory.org.uk

YORKSHIRE – NORTH RIDING

Cleveland, N. Yorkshire & S. Durham FHS
CONTACT: Mr A. Sampson, 1 Oxgang Close, Redcar,
Cleveland TS10 4ND
w: www.clevelandfhs.org.uk/

YORKSHIRE – WEST RIDING

Barnsley FHS
CONTACT: Gail Woodhead, 4 Cranford Gardens, Royston, Barnsley
S71 4SP
e: secretary@barnsleyfhs.co.uk
w: www.barnsleyfhs.co.uk

Bradford FHS
CONTACT: Carol Duckworth, 5 Leaventhorpe Avenue,
Fairweather Green, Bradford BD8 0ED
e: secretary@bradfordfhs.org.uk
w: www.bradfordfhs.org.uk

Calderdale FHS (incorporating Halifax & District)
CONTACT: Anne Whitaker, 13 Far View Illingworth, Halifax, W Yorks
e: secretary@cfhsw.co.uk
w: www.cfhsw.co.uk

Doncaster & District FHS
CONTACT: Mrs M Staniforth, 5 Breydon Avenue, Cusworth,
Doncaster, S Yorks, DN5 8JZ
e: secretary@doncasterfhs.co.uk
w: www.doncasterfhs.co.uk

Harrogate & District FHS
CONTACT: Mrs Wendy Symington, 18 Aspin Drive, Knaresborough,
N Yorks HG5 8HH

Huddersfield & District FHS
CONTACT: Alan Stewart-Kaye, 63 Dunbottle Lane, Mirfield, W Yorks
WF14 9JJ
e: secretary@hdfhs.org.uk
w: www.hdfhs.org.uk

Keighley & District FHS
CONTACT: Mrs S. Daynes, 2 The Hallowes, Shann Park, Keighley,
W Yorks BD20 6HY
w: www.keighleyfamilyhistory.org.uk

Morley & District FH Group
CONTACT: Mrs Carol Sklinar, 1 New Lane, East Ardsley, Wakefield
WF3 2DP
e: carol@morleyfhg.co.uk
w: www.morleyfhg.co.uk

Pontefract & District FHS
CONTACT: Mrs Glynis Tate, Eadon House, Main Street, Hensall,
Goole DN14 0QZ
e: secretary@pontefractfhs.org.uk
w: www.pontefractfhs.org.uk

Ripon Historical Society & FHG
CONTACT: Mrs Mary Moseley, 42 Knox Avenue, Harrogate, N Yorks
HG1 3JB
w: www.yorksgen.co.uk/rh/rh1.htm

Rotherham FHS
CONTACT: Brian Allott, Secretary Rotherham FHS, 36 Warren Hill,
Rotherham, S Yorks S61 3SX
e: secretary@rotherhamfhs.co.uk
w: www.rotherhamfhs.co.uk

Selby FHS
CONTACT: Marilyn Newall, Keswick House, Kelfield Road, Riccall,
York YO19 6PG
e: m_newall@hotmail.com
w: www.geocities.com/selbyfamilyhistory/

Sheffield & District FHS
CONTACT: Mrs Diane Maskell, 5 Old Houses, Piccadilly Road,
Chesterfield S61 0EH
e: secretary@sheffieldfhs.org.uk
w: www.sheffieldfhs.org.uk

Wakefield & District FHS
CONTACT: Kathy Wattie, Secretary Wakefield & District FHS,
12 Malting Rise, Robin Hood, Wakefield, W Yorks WF3 3AY
e: secretary@wdfhs.co.uk
w: www.wdfhs.co.uk

Wharfedale FHG
CONTACT: Mrs Susan Hartley, 1 West View Court, Yeadon, Leeds
LS19 7HX
e: hon.secretary@wfhg.org.uk
w: www.yorksgen.co.uk/wfhg/wfhg.htm

WALES

Association of Family History Societies of Wales
CONTACT: Geoff Riggs, Peacehaven, Badgers Meadow, Pwllmeyric,
Chepstow, Mon NP16 6UE
e: secretary@fhswales.info
w: www.fhswales.info

ANGLESEY
Gwynedd FHS
CONTACT: J Bryan Jones, Secretary Gwynedd FHS, 7 Victoria Road,
Old Colwyn, Conwy LL29 9SN
e: bryan.jones8@btinternet.com
w: www.gwyneddfhs.org

BRECONSHIRE (OR BRECKNOCKSHIRE)
Powys FHS
CONTACT: Keith Morgan, Drefach, Siluria, Walton, Presteigne, Powys
DL8 2RE
e: kmor@kmor.wanadoo.co.uk
w: www.rootsw.com/~wlspfhs/

CAERNARVONSHIRE
Gwynedd FHS
CONTACT: J Bryan Jones, Secretary Gwynedd FHS, 7 Victoria Road, Old Colwyn, Conwy LL29 9SN

CARDIGANSHIRE
Cardiganshire FHS
CONTACT: Menna H Evans, Cardiganshire FHS, Adran Casgliadau, c/o National Library of Wales, Aberystwyth, Ceredigion SY23 3BU
e: sec@cgnfhs.org.uk
w: www.cgnfhs.org.uk

Dyfed FHS
CONTACT:Mrs. Beti Williams, 12 Elder Grove, Llamgunnor, Carmarthen, Carmarthenshire SA31 2LQ
e: secretary@dyfedfhs.org.uk
w: www.dyfedfhs.org.uk

CARMARTHENSHIRE
Dyfed FHS
CONTACT: Mrs. Beti Williams, 12 Elder Grove, Llamgunnor, Carmarthen, Carmarthenshire SA31 2LQ
e: secretary@dyfedfhs.org.uk
w: www.dyfedfhs.org.uk

DENBIGHSHIRE & FLINTSHIRE
Clwyd FHS
CONTACT: Mrs A Anderson, The Laurels, Dolydd Road, Cefn Mawr, Wrexham LL14 3NH
w: www.clwydfhs.org.uk

GLAMORGAN
Glamorgan FHS
CONTACT: Mrs R Williams, 93 Pwllygath Street, Bridgend CF36 6ET
e: secretary@glamfhs.org
w: www.glamfhs.org

MERIONETHSHIRE
Gwynedd FHS
CONTACT:J Bryan Jones, Secretary Gwynedd FHS, 7 Victoria Road, Old Colwyn, Conwy LL29 9SN

MONMOUTHSHIRE
Gwent FHS
CONTACT: Hon. Secretary, 11 Rosser St, Wainfelin, Pontypool NP4 6EA
e: secretary@gwentfhs.info
w: www.gwentfhs.info

MONTGOMERYSHIRE
Powys FHS
CONTACT: Keith Morgan, Drefach, Siluria, Walton, Presteigne, Powys
DL8 2RE
e: kmor@kmor.wanadoo.co.uk
w: www.rootsw.com/~wlspfhs/

Montgomeryshire GS
CONTACT: Mrs, Sue Harrison-Stone, Cambrian House,
Brimmon Lane, Newtown, Montgomeryshire, Powys SY16 1BY
e: sue_powys@hotmail.com
w: www.home.freeuk.net/montgensoc

PEMBROKESHIRE
Dyfed FHS
CONTACT: Mrs. Beti Williams, 12 Elder Grove, Llamgunnor,
Carmarthen, Carmarthenshire SA31 2LQ
e: secretary@dyfedfhs.org.uk
w: www.dyfedfhs.org.uk

RADNORSHIRE
Powys FHS
CONTACT: Keith Morgan, Drefach, Siluria, Walton, Presteigne, Powys
DL8 2RE
e: kmor@kmor.wanadoo.co.uk
w: www.rootsw.com/~wlspfhs/

SCOTLAND

The Scottish Association of Family History Societies
Aberdeen and North East Scotland Family History Society
The Hon. Secretary, The Family History Shop, 164 King Street,
Aberdeen AB24 5BD
T: 01224 646323, Fax: 01224 639096
e: enquiries@anesfhs.org.uk
w: www.anesfhs.org.uk/

Alloway & Southern Ayrshire Family History Society
The Hon. Secretary, c/o Alloway Library,
Doonholm Road, Ayr KA7 4QQ
e: asafhs@mtcharlesayr.fsnet.co.uk
w: www.asafhs.co.uk

Anglo Scottish Family History Society
Clayton House, 59 Piccadily, Manchester M1 2AQ

Association of Scottish Genealogists and Researchers in Archives (ASGRA)
The Hon. Secretary, 93 Colinton Road, Edinburgh EH4 1ET
e: hazelweir@sea-insite.org.uk
w: www.asgra.co.uk

Borders Family History Society
Hon. Secretary, Ronald Morrison, Buchan Cottage, Duns Castle, Duns
TD11 3NW
w: www.bordersfhs.org.uk

Caithness Family History Society
Hon Secretary, Mr. Sandy Gunn, 9 Provost Cormack Drive, Thurso,
Caithness KW14 7ES
e: sandy.gunn@btinternet.com
w: www.caithnessfhs.org.uk

Central Scotland Family History Society
The Hon. Secretary, 11 Springbank Gardens, Dunblane FK15 9JX
w: www.csfhs.org.uk/

Dumfries and Galloway Family History Society
The Hon. Secretary, Family History Centre, 9 Glasgow Street, Dumfries
DG2 9AF
e: secretary@dgfhs.org.uk
w: www.dgfhs.org.uk

East Ayrshire Family History Society
The Hon. Secretary c/o The Dick Institute, Elmbank Ave, Kilmarnock
KA1 3BU
e: enquiries@eastayrshirefhs.org.uk
w: www.eastayrshirefhs.org.uk/

Fife Family History Society
The Hon. Secretary, Glenmoriston, Durie Street Leven, Fife KY8 4HF
e: wadmin@fifefhs.org
w: www.fifefhs.org

Glasgow & West of Scotland Family History Society
The Hon. Secretary, Unit 13, 32 Mansfield Street, Glasgow G11 5QP
w: www.gwsfhs.org.uk/

Highland Family History Society
The Hon. Secretary, c/o Reference Room, Public Library, Farraline Park,
Inverness IV1 INH
e: jdurham@highlandfhs.org.uk
w: www.highlandfhs.org.uk

Lanarkshire Family History Society
Hon. Secretary, 26A Motherwell Business Centre, Coursington Road,
Motherwell, Lanarkshire ML1 1PW
e: info@lanarkshirefhs.org.uk or society@lanarkshirefhs.org.uk
w: www.lanarkshirefhs.org.uk

Largs and North Ayrshire Family History Society
c/o Largs Library, 18 Allanpark Street, Largs KA30 9AG
w: www.largsnafhs.org.uk/home.htm

Orkney Family History Society
Hon. Secretary, Orkney FHS., Orkney Library & Archive,
44 Junction Road, Kirkwall, Orkney KW15 1HG

Renfrewshire Family History Society
The Hon. Secretary, PO Box 9239, Kilmacolm PA13 4WZ
w: www.renfrewshirefhs.co.uk

SCOTSLOT
Chairman: Mrs Elizabeth van Lottum, 16 Bloomfield Road, Harpenden
Herts AL5 4DB

Shetland Family History Society
The Hon. Secretary, 6 Hillhead, Lerwick, Shetland ZE1 0EJ
e: secretary@shetland-fhs.org.uk
w: www.shetland-fhs.org.uk

Tay Valley Family History Society covering the former Counties of
Angus, Fife, Kinross & Perth
The Hon. Secretary, Research Centre, 179-181 Princes Street, Dundee
DD4 6DQ
T: 01382 461845
e: tvfhs@tayvalleyfhs.org.uk
w: www.tayvalleyfhs.org.uk

The Genealogy Society of Utah
Family History Support Office, 185 Penns Lane, Sutton Coalfield,
West Midlands B75 1JU
w: www.familysearch.org/

The Heraldry Society of Scotland
The Hon Secratary , 22 Craigentinny Crescent, Edinburgh EH7 6QA
e: c.napier@napier.aol.com.uk
w: www.heraldry-scotland.co.uk

The Lothian Family History Society
The Hon. Secretary, c/o Lasswade High School Centre, , Eskdale Drive,
Bonnyrigg, Midlothian EH19 2LA
e: lothiansfhs@hotmail.com
w: www.lothiansfhs.org.uk

The Scottish Genealogy Society
The Hon. Secretary, Library and Family History Centre,
15 Victoria Terrace, Edinburgh EH1 2JL
T: 0131 220 3677
e: sales@scotsgenealogy.com
w: www.scotsgenealogy.com

Troon @ Ayrshire Family History Society
The Hon. Secretary, c/o M.E.R.C. Troon Public Library, , South Beach,
Troon, Ayrshire KA10 6EF
e: info@troonayrshirefhs.org.uk
w: www.troonayrshirefhs.org.uk

West Lothian Family History Society
Hon. Secretary, 23 Templar Rise, Livingstone EH54 6PJ
e: honsec@wlfhs.org.uk
w: www.wlfhs.org.uk

AUSTRALIA

Australasian Federation of Family History Organisations Inc
CONTACT: PO Box 3012 Weston Creek ACT 2611 Australia
E: secretary@affho.org
w: www.affho.org/

Australian Institute of Gen Studies Inc
CONTACT: PO Box 339, Blackburn, Victoria 3130, Australia
e: info@aigs.org.au
w: www.aigs.org.au

Blue Mountains Family History Society
CONTACT: Mrs Suzanne Voytas, Secretary, Blue Mountains FHS Inc,
PO Box 97, Springwood, New South Wales 2777, Australia
e: exploretree@yahoo.com.au
w: www.rootsw.com/~nswbmfhs/activities.htm

Botany Bay FHS Inc
CONTACT: Botany Bay FHS Inc, PO Box 1006, Sutherland,
New South Wales 1499, Australia
e: botanybayfhs@yahoo.com.au
w: au.geocities.com/bbfhs

Cape Banks FHS Inc
CONTACT: PO Box 67, Maroubra, New South Wales 2035, Australia
e: hazelb@compassnet.com.au
w: www.capebanks.org.au

Cairns & District FHS Inc
CONTACT: Mrs Beverley O'Hara, PO Box 5069, Cairns,
Queensland 4870, Australia
e: rondac@ozemail.com.au
w: cwpp.slq.qld.gov.au/cdfhs

Central Queensland FH Association Inc
CONTACT: CQFHA, PO Box 6000, Rockhampton Mail Centre,
Queensland 4701, Australia
e: cqfha@hotmail.com
w: www.rootsw.com/~auscqfha

Central Coast FHS Inc
CONTACT: PO Box 4090, East Gosford, New South Wales 2250,
Australia
e: secretary@centralcoastfhs.org.au
w: www.centralcoastfhs.org.au

Dubbo & District FHS Inc
CONTACT: PO Box 868, Dubbo, New South Wales 2830, Australia
e: ddfhs_2000@yahoo.com.au
w: www.au.geocities.com/ddfhs_2000

Genealogical Soc of the Northern Territory Inc
CONTACT: Mrs June Tomlinson, PO Box 37212, Winnellie,
Northern Territory 0821, Australia

Genealogical Soc of Queensland Inc
CONTACT: PO Box 8423, Woolloongabba, Queensland 4102, Australia
e: gsq@gsq.org.au
w: www.gsq.org.au

Gold Coast Family History Society Inc
CONTACT: PO Box 2763, Southport, Queensland 4215, Australia
e: annmorse@ozemail.com.au
w: www.members.ozemail.com.au/~annmorse/nerang.html

Illawarra FHG
CONTACT: Mrs K. Alexander, PO Box 1652, South Coast Mail Centre,
Wollongong, New South Wales 2521, Australia
w: www.rootsw.com/~ausifhg/

Lithgow & District FHS Inc
CONTACT: PO Box 516, Lithgow, New South Wales 2790, Australia
e: ldfhs@lisp.com.au
w: www.lisp.com.au/~ldfhs

Maryborough District FHS Inc
CONTACT: PO Box 408, Maryborough, Queensland, 4650, Australia
e: mdfhs@satcom.net.au
w: www.satcom.net.au/mdfhs

Moruya & District Historical Society Inc
CONTACT: PO Box 259, Moruya, New South Wales 2537, Australia

Nepean FHS Inc
CONTACT: PO Box 81, Emu Plains, New South Wales 2750, Australia

Newcastle FHS Inc
CONTACT: The Secretary, NFHS Inc, PO Box 189, Adamstown,
New South Wales 2289, Australia
w: www.ozemail.com.au/~ahgw/nfhs

Orange FHS
CONTACT: PO Box 930, Orange, New South Wales 2800, Australia

Queensland FHS Inc
CONTACT: PO Box 171, Indooroopilly, Brisbane, Queensland 4068,
Australia
e: info@qfhs.org.au
w: www.qfhs.org.au

Richmond-Tweed FHS
CONTACT: The Secretary, PO Box 817, Ballina, New South Wales
2478, Australia

South Australian Gen & Her Soc Inc
CONTACT: Mr Dale Johns, GPO Box 592, Adelaide, South Australia
5001, Australia
e: info@saghs.org.au
w: www.saghs.org.au

Soc of Australian Genealogists
CONTACT: Richmond Villa, 120 Kent Street, Observatory Hill,
Sydney, New South Wales 2000, Australia
e: info@sag.org.au
w: www.sag.org.au

Scottish Ancestry Group, Genealogical Society of Victoria Inc.
Hon. Secretary, Level 6, 179 Queen Street, Melbourne,
Victoria 3000, Australia
e: gsv@gsv.org.au
w: www.gsv.org.au

Scottish Interest Group, Genealogical Society of Queensland Inc.
Hon. Secretary, P.O. Box 8423 Woolloongabba, Queensland, 4102, Australia
e: gsq@gsq.org.au
w: www.gsq.org.au

Scottish Interest Group, Western Australian Genealogical Society
6/48 May Street, Bayswater, Western Australia 6053, Australia
e: genealogy@wags.org.au
w: www.wags.org.au

Shoalhaven FHS
CONTACT: Robyn Burke, P.O. Box 591, Nowra, New South Wales
2541, Australia

Society of Australian Genealogists
Richmond Villa, 120 Kent Street, Sydney, NSW 2000, Australia
e: info@sag.org.au
w: www.sag.org.au

South Australia Genealogy & Heraldry Society Inc
Hon.Secretary, PO Box 592, Adelaide, SA 5001, Australia
e: admin@saghs.org.au
w: www.saghs.org.au

Tasmanian FHS Inc
formerly Genealogical Society of Tasmania, prior to 01APR2001
CONTACT: Mrs Betty Bissett, PO Box 191, Launceston, Tasmania 7250,
Australia
e: secretary@tasfhs.org
w: www.tasfhs.org/

The Genealogical Soc of Victoria Inc
CONTACT: 6th Floor, 179 Queen Street, Melbourne,
Victoria 3000, Australia
e: gsv@gsv.org.au
w: www.gsv.org.au

The Heraldry & Genealogy Soc of Canberra Inc
CONTACT: GPO Box 585, Canberra, Australian Capital Territory
2601, Australia
e: hagsoc@hagsoc.org.au
w: www.hagsoc.org.au

Tweed Gold Coast FH & Heritage Association
CONTACT: PO Box 266, Tweed Heads, New South Wales 2485,
Australia
e: tweedfhs@hotmail.com
w: www.geocities.com/twintownsfamilyhistory/

Wagga Wagga & District FHS
CONTACT: PO Box 307, Wagga Wagga, New South Wales 2650, Australia
e: rivtron@bigpond.com
w: www.wsg.net.au/wagga

Western Australian Gen Soc Inc
CONTACT: Unit 6, 48 May Street, Bayswater, Western Australia 6053,
Australia
e: genealogy@wags.org.au
w: www.wags.org.au

CANADA

Alberta Family Histories Soc
CONTACT: 712-16 Avenue NW, Calgary, Alberta T2M 0J8, Canada
e: afhs@afhs.ab.ca
w: www.afhs.ab.ca

Alberta Genealogical Soc
CONTACT: #116, 10440-108 Avenue, Edmonton, Alberta T5H 3Z9,
Canada
e: agsoffice@compusmart.ab.ca
w: http://abgensoc.ca/

British Isles Family History Society of Greater Ottawa
P.O. Box 38026, Ottawa, Ontario K2C 3Y7, Canada
e: queries@bifhsgo.ca
w: www.bifhsgo.ca

Ontario Gen.Society (Kingston Branch)
CONTACT: The Corresponding Secretary, Post Office Box 1394,
Kingston, Ontario K7L 5C6, Canada
w: http://w.ctsolutions.com/ogskingston/

Ontario Gen.Society (Toronto Branch)
CONTACT: Paul Jones, Ontario Genealogical Society, Toronto Branch,
Box 518, Station K, Toronto, Ontario, M4P 2G9, Canada
e: pauljones@rogers.com
w: www.torontofamilyhistory.org

Quebec FHS
CONTACT: PO Box 1026, Postal Station Pointe Claire, Quebec
H9S 4H9, Canada
e: admin@qfhs.ca
w: www.qfhs.ca

Saskatchewan Genealogical Soc
CONTACT: 2nd Floor, 1870 Lorne Street, P.O. Box 1894, Regina,
Saskatchewan S4P 3E1, Canada
w: www.saskgenealogy.com

The British Columbia Gen Soc
CONTACT: PO Box 88054, Lansdowne, Richmond, British Columbia
V6X 3T6, Canada
e: bcgs@bcgs.ca
w: www.bcgs.ca/

Victoria Genealogical Soc
CONTACT: PO Box 43021, RPO Victoria North, Victoria,
BC V8X 3G2, Canada
e: vgs@victoriags.org
w: www.victoriags.org

NEW ZEALAND

New Zealand FHS Inc
CONTACT: Mrs J. Lord, PO Box 13301, Armagh, Christchurch,
New Zealand
e: reasearch@xtra.co.nz

New Zealand Society of Genealogists Inc.
P.O. Box 8795, Symonds Street, Auckland 1035, New Zealand
e: nzsg-contact@genealogy.org.nz
w: www.genealogy.org.nz

UNITED STATES

British Isles FHS – USA
CONTACT: Secretary, 2531 Sawtelle Blvd, PMB 134, Los Angeles, CA
90064-3124, USA
w: www.rootsw.com/~bifhsusa

Federation of Genealogical Societies
CONTACT: PO Box 200940, Austin, TX 78720-0940, USA
e: fgs-office@fgs.org
w: www.fgs.org

Genealogical Society of Pennsylvania
CONTACT: 215 S. Broad St, 7th Floor, Philadelphia, PA 19107-5325, USA
e: gsppa@aol.com
w: www.genpa.org

International Society for British Genealogy & Family History
CONTACT: PO Box 350459, Westminster, CO 80035-0459, USA
e: isbgfh@yahoo.com
w: www.isbgfh.org

Santa Barbara County Gen Soc
CONTACT: PO Box 1303, Goleta, CA 93116-1303, USA
e: sbcgs@msn.com
w: www.cagenw.com/santabarbara/sbcgs/

OTHER SOCIETIES

Anglo-German FHS
CONTACT: Mr Peter Towey, 20 Skylark Rise, Woolwell, Plymouth, Devon PL6 7SN

Anglo-Italian FHS
CONTACT: Elaine Collins (Chairman) 3 Calais Street, London, SE5 9LP
e: chairman@anglo-italianfhs.org.uk
w: www.anglo-italianfhs.org.uk

British Association for Cemeteries in S. Asia
CONTACT: Mr T. Wilkinson MBE, 76 $\frac{1}{2}$ Chartfield Avenue, London SW15 6HQ

British Record Society
CONTACT: Mrs C. Busfield, Stone Barn Farm, Sutherland Road, Longsdon, Staffs ST9 9QD
e: britishrecordsociety@hotmail.com
w: http://britishrecordsociety.org.uk

Catholic FHS
CONTACT: Mrs Margaret Bowery, 9 Snows Green Road, Shotley Bridge, Consett, Co. Durham DH8 0HD
w: www.catholic-history.org.uk/cfhs/index.htm

Genealogical Society of Utah (UK)
CONTACT: Mr.G.D.Mawlam, 185 Penns Lane, Sutton Coldfield, West Midlands B76 1JU
The Institute of Heraldic & Genealogical Studies
CONTACT: Mr J. Palmer, Northgate, Canterbury, Kent CT1 1 BA
e: ihgs@ihgs.ac.uk
w: www.ihgs.ac.uk

Jewish Genealogical Society of Great Britain
CONTACT: Mr A Winner, PO Box 13288, London N3 3WD
e: enquiries@jgsgb.org.uk
w: www.jgsgb.org.uk/

Krans-Buckland Family Association
CONTACT: Mrs J. Buckland, PO Box 1025, North Highlands,
California 95660-1025, USA
e: jkbfa@sbcglobal.net

Pedigree Users Group
CONTACT: Malcolm Austen, 11 Corn Avill Close, Abingdon, Oxford
OX14 2ND
e: chairman@pugw.org.uk
w: www.pugw.org.uk

Quaker FHS
CONTACT: Mrs Liz Butler, 3 Sheridan Place, Hampton, Middlesex
TW12 2SB
e: info@qfhs.co.uk
w: www.qfhs.co.uk

Railway Ancestors FHS
CONTACT: Mr Jeremy Engert, Lundy, King Edward St, Barmouth,
Gwynedd LL42 1NY
w: www.railwayancestors.fsnet.co.uk

Romany & Traveller FHS
CONTACT: Mrs J. Keet-Black, 6 St.James Walk, South Chailey,
East Sussex BN8 4BU
w: www.rtfhs.org.uk

Society of Genealogists
CONTACT: 14 Charterhouse Buildings, Goswell Road, London EC1M 7BA
e: genealogy@sog.org.uk
w: www.sog.org.uk

The Association of Genealogists and Researchers in Archives (AGRA)
CONTACT: Mr David Young, 29 Badgers Close, Horsham, West Sussex
RH12 5RU
e: agra@agra.org.uk
w: www.agra.org.uk

The Families in British India Society
CONTACT: Mr Peter Bailey, Sentosa, Godolphin Rd, Weybridge, Surrey
KT13 0PT
w: www.fibis.org